Blogging

Special Edition – Two Books

Make Money Blogging

Quickly Set Up Your Own Money Making Blog Site Using WordPress (FREE)

Peter Cole

Blogging

Special Edition – Two Books in One

Published by:

CyberLearners, LLC.
Cleveland, Ohio

Book One

Make Money Blogging

How to Set Up a Blog On Your Own Self-Hosted Domain and Make Money

How to Get to Five-Figures in Five Months

Lee Sebastian

Published By:

Colonial Publishing
Cleveland, Ohio

Legal Disclaimer

The author of this book has taken careful measures to share vital information about the subject. May its readers acquire the right knowledge, wisdom, inspiration, and succeed.

Table of Contents

Introduction

I started my first blog site with a Netscape HTML editor in 1998. Back then it was very easy to get to number 1 or 2 in the search results with AltaVista, Yahoo and InfoSeek in a matter of 2-3 days. There were all sorts of crazy hacks you could also do to trick the algorithms. Things have obviously changed A LOT in 20 years.

In 2012 I finally transitioned over to WordPress, from running static HTML websites. It was a major "aha" moment for me as I realized how much more easy it was going to be run a blog using WordPress. Previously I was doing all the development work, manually coding individual HTML web pages, forms, scripts, then uploading. It was a very exhausting process.

The biggest key to monetizing a blog is how good your article posts are and your SEO. SEO is paramount in getting a high quality score with any search engine now. Your articles need to be dynamic, linked, integrated with social media, YouTube, extremely relevant and original...WHY?

Because, quite simply; Google and the other search engines have become so good at analyzing and ranking content, it is basically A.I. doing all of this now, you can't trick it. The technology is growing so fast and becoming so smart, if you can't keep up then you will get left behind.

So this is good if you are very motivated but not so good if you are lazy. Expect a large amount of "hobby bloggers" to be cancelled out by this new and expanding web technology.

If you can excel in a niche that you are passionate about and not get tired creating good content on, especially videos, then you can succeed in monetizing your blog site. In addition, the skills you will obtain from becoming an expert blogger (SEO, Wordpress platform, Content writing, online ads) will place you in a great position as well.

I highly recommend any blogger use WordPress as their platform because of the plugins you can use to enhance your site, especially the Yoast SEO plugin. Plus, most web developers are familiar with WordPress platform

Chapter One
Blogging 101

What is a blog?

Blogging is very popular these days. You can think of any topic that you want, and you will most likely find blogs about it. In fact, any research you do on a search engine is going to result in mostly informational blog sites that get relevant traffic and monetize that traffic in some form or fashion.

But, what exactly is a blog? You can think of a blog as some kind of online journal or diary. Blogging allows you complete freedom of what you want to write about. Not only that, since blogging exists online, you also get to share your work with the whole world. People who love to travel will most likely write travel blogs; people who like clothes might end up making a fashion blog. The thing is that you can blog about anything and everything. The sky is the limit. A good tip is to blog about something that you are personally interested in since blogs are expected to be active and need to be regularly updated.

You might be wondering if there is a difference between a blog and a website. It should be noted that a blog *is* a website, but not all websites can be considered a blog. Blogs tend to be less formal and are regularly updated, about at least once a week. Blogs also tend to have a lot of engagement with readers.

A person who writes a blog is called a blogger, and the act of writing a blog is called blogging. There are countless blogs around the world, and more and more blogs are being added.

People blog for various reasons. Many bloggers simply want to share their interests, while there are those who just want to entertain. There are also those who blog to make money. Indeed, blogging can be a great source of passive income. The truth is that you can blog for whatever reason you might have. In fact, you can also blog for no reason.

Blogging is an effective way of sharing something with the world. It can also be a fun activity. In fact, there are bloggers out there who simply enjoy blogging and give almost no interest in earning money from what they are doing. But, of course, blogging can also be used to generate a good flow of cash.

It should be noted that blogging also has its challenges. Gone are the days when you can expect your blog to draw lots of followers, even if you just write about anything. The blogging industry has become more competitive. For your blog to be a success, then you need to apply the right techniques and effective practices. Do not worry; by the time you finish reading this book, you will definitely be ready to create a blog that will generate a decent amount of profits.

As you can see, blogging is not just about sharing what you love with the world; it will also allow you to get paid to write and share your interests. This is one of the best things about blogging. It is also worth mentioning that blogging can be a very fun and addicting activity. In fact, there are people out there who regularly spend hours working on their blog. If you are serious about becoming a successful blogger, then you should be ready to put in the time and effort to work on and improve your blog, NON-STOP.

A blog also allows you to meet people, especially those who

have the same interests as the subject of your blog. It is not uncommon for established blogs to generate thousands of blogs in a single day. People also like to leave comments and engage with blog posts.

Now, the value of a blog depends on the blogger. If you fill your blog with quality contents, then even other people will perceive your blog to be of value and importance. However, if you just fill it with fluff contents, then your blog can be said to have little to no value. Simply, your blog is what you make of it.

Why blogging for profit is the best long-term strategy for making money online.

When it comes to making money online, blogging is the most popular and probably the best option that you have. However, do not expect to make money from blogging overnight. It takes time for a blog to get established. However, do not be discouraged. Once your blog is already well established, then you can expect a steady stream of income. Successful blogs generate money on their own. Imagine doing what you love, writing about the subject that you are interested in, and making money from it. This is what it is like to have a successful blog. But then again, take note that achieving this kind of success does not happen overnight. You also need to dedicate time and effort into your blog.

If you want to make money with your blog, you should view it more as a long-term strategy than something that you do within a short period. This is another reason why you should only blog about something that you are personally interested in. **Indeed, it is not easy to write about things that you do not even like to talk about.**

Unlike other things online that soon fade, a blog gets even more established over time as long as you stick to the best practices of blogging. Blogging is never really meant to be a short-term strategy. Hence, if you just want to write a few lines or articles and cannot expound on your subject, then perhaps you should pick a different subject to blog about. Do not worry; there are many ways to expound on a subject. You simply have to view it from different angles and make your own reflections and realizations. If you do this, you will be surprised at just how much you can write about and tackle on the same subject.

When you start to earn from your blog, you will most likely notice just a few dollars trickle in the first few weeks or months. However, as your blog gets more established over time, you will see significant increases in your income. The good thing is that as your blog gets more established, the less work you have to do.

There are also many other ways to earn money once you have a well-established blog. This is why blogging is the best long-term strategy to make money online. The longer you blog and the more established it becomes, the more money you can make.

Is it possible to earn a six-figure income in five months? Well, the answer is yes. However, do not expect for it to be easy. These days, blogging has become very competitive. There are also many new blogs that get created every day. The good news is that among the countless of blogs out there, only a few bloggers really know how to blog properly. This is your strong edge against the rising competition. However, you need to take positive actions. Remember that blogging is not just about knowing but is, in fact, more about doing. So, by the time you finish reading this book, grab your laptop and start blogging.

How much money can you make?

So, just how much money can you earn by blogging? There is no hard and fast rule on this matter. Some bloggers do not earn anything from their blogs, while there are many who only earn a few dollars. However, there are those who earn a high amount of income, so much so that they are able to leave their office job and blog full time. When you engage in blogging, the amount of money that you make usually depends on how much time and effort that you put into it. Of course, it is also important that you know the best practices and important techniques that will make your blog work.

If you have a new blog, you should not expect to make any money from it. Again, you should keep in mind that blogging is a long-term strategy. Many bloggers stop in the first few weeks because they get discouraged for not earning any money. However, do not let this happen to you. Instead of being discouraged, you should simply continue writing and updating your blog.

There is no strict rule as to the timeline on when you can start earning from your blog. It usually starts with just a few dollars, but then increases over time as our blog gets more traffic and followers. Patience and perseverance are very important qualities to have if you want to be a successful blogger. The sad truth is that more than 65% of bloggers fail to earn as much income as they would like to. Now, do not include yourself in this 65% who fail to make any money. This is because most of these people are those who also lack the knowledge of how to properly manage a blog. To be a successful blogger, there are two important elements that you should keep in mind: You have to acquire the right knowledge, and you also need to put that knowledge into actual practice.

Biggest Drivers of Blog Success

- Your SEO Skills for attracting organic Traffic
- Your skills in online advertising
- Creating relevant and engaging posts, articles and videos
- Integrating social media 100%
- Making sure your site is constantly optimized for search engines
- Your site load speed and engaging structure
- Monetizing your traffic with CPA action ads like Google AdSense.
- Bottom line; getting a following in a niche.

It is noteworthy that money is not the only reason why people write blogs. In fact, there are also many bloggers out there who continue to blog even though they do not earn any money from it. To them, it is not financial gain that they are after but just the activity of blogging that gives them a sense of joy. Indeed, blogging can be a very fun activity. In fact, it is so easy to get drawn and addicted to it.

Here is a common question: Can you make a living even if you have one successful blog? Well, the answer is a resounding *yes*. The truth is that you do not have to create multiple blogs to be successful. Although there are bloggers who manage several blogs at the same time, know that it is also possible to earn a full-time income even with just one blog. When it comes to blogging, there is simply no limit to how much you can earn. You can earn as little as you want and as much as you want. The sky is the limit. But, of course, if you want to earn more money, then you also need to do more and be more committed to your blog. Do not worry; creating a successful blog does not mean that you need to spend hours working on it. There are many successful people out there who earn a decent amount of money from their blog, even though they only blog during their free time. Just remember to blog regularly.

It is not just the amount of money that you can earn that makes blogging so attractive, but it also allows you to earn money by being your own boss. What is more, if you like the subject of your blog, then this will allow you to earn a huge amount if income simply by talking about something that you are interested in. So, how much money can you make? Well, you can name your price. You decide, and remember to accompany it with positive actions.

Is it for you?

Is blogging for you? Well, only you can answer this question. Is there anything that you want to write about and share with the world? Are you willing to dedicate time and effort to your blog? If your answer is yes, especially to the second question, then there is a good chance that you can be a successful blogger.

The truth is that it is hard to tell if blogging is right for you just by thinking about it. There are those who try it out <u>and only then do they realize that they enjoy the activities of a blogger.</u> There are also those who are so eager to start only to realize somewhere along the way that they are not willing to spend the efforts to work on their blog. Although you can blog just for fun or as a hobby, you should know that if you want to make money with your blog, then you definitely need to give it time and effort. Just like anything that is worth pursuing, establishing a blog also requires some dedication and commitment on your part. This is true, especially if you intend to make money from your blog.

Now, the only way to tell if blogging is for you is simply to give it a try. A good way to do this is to use a free blogging platform like *blogger*. This will help give you an actual feel of what it is to blog without having to spend any real money. Now, if you strongly feel like you really want to blog, then you can skip this step and proceed to make a real and professional blog. Creating a professional blog is discussed in the next chapter.

So, what are you waiting for? You should stop thinking and simply start blogging to find out if blogging is for you. Sometimes the only way to find out if this will work for you or not is by giving it a try.

Now, can you still blog even if you do not like to write? Well, this is a legitimate question. After all, not all people enjoy writing. There are many people out there who know a lot but are simply too lazy or busy to put their thoughts into writing. So, is it still possible to blog even if you are not fond of writing? The answer to this question is *yes*. In fact, there are many bloggers out there who earn a decent income from their blog even though they have not written anything. How does this happen? Well, if you are not fond of writing, yet still want to blog, then you can hire ghostwriters to do all the writing work for you. What is a ghostwriter? It is a writer who will write your content or book but will not take any credit for it. This means that you remain as the sole owner and author of the work of the ghostwriter; they will write your content and disappear. No, they will not take any credit over the work as long as you pay them. Think of ghostwriters as writers for hire who do not claim any ownership over their work. However, the problem with hiring a ghostwriter is that it can get expensive in the long run, especially if you work with a real professional ghostwriter who value his/her work. Still, it is noteworthy that there are people out there who make money without having written anything on their own, but merely rely on the works of a ghostwriter. In the world of ghostwriting, you will usually receive the same quality of work as the payment that you have been charged. Hence, the general rule is that if you want to have high-quality work, then you should be ready to spend a much higher amount. Do not worry; you can try to recover all of your expenses from the book sales.

The only way to know if blogging is for you is to do it. There are no shortcuts or sound advice to be given. Just do it and see what happens.

Chapter Two

Create a Blog

A Step-by-Step Guide to Creating your Blog

Now that you have a good understanding of what blogging is all about, it is time for you to learn how to create your blog. Creating a blog can be a daunting task, especially if you do not know what you are doing. This guide will simplify things and lead you through every step of the process of blog creation. Do not rush the learning process. Take as much time to understand the steps and be sure to execute them properly. Do not worry; the truth is that the process of creating a blog should not be difficult. Just stick to the teachings in this book, and you will be on your way to having a brand new blog that you can enjoy.

Why do you want to blog?

Okay, before you take the joy and responsibility of being a blog owner, you should ask and make it clear to yourself: Why do you want to have a blog? Is it to share something that you are passionate about with the world, or do you also want to make money with it, or maybe you want both? Knowing your reasons for blogging is important so that you will know the approach that you will take. Of course, if you only want to blog as a hobby or in your free time, then perhaps you do not need to exert too much effort into making your blog; however, if you really want to be a real blogger and want to earn something serious with it, then you need to give enough time and commitment to your blog. Knowing your reasons for blogging will also give you a sense of direction as well as inspiration.

Select your niche/passion

When creating a blog, it is strongly advised that you blog about something that you are personally interested in as your niche. What is it that drives you and makes you feel passionate about? It is also important that you identify a specific niche. Gone are the days when you can just blog about anything you want. The blogging industry is much more competitive than you might think. Before you even start to create a blog, you should identify the specific topic of your blog. For example, if your blog is about health, what is it about health that you want to talk about? Will it be a blog about losing weight, or will it be about natural remedies? You can even make it more specific by identifying the specific remedy illness that you want to write about. The more specific your blog is, the more targeted it will be.

Of course, it is still possible to make a blog that covers a wide range of topics and sub-topics. However, take note that many experts suggest that it is now better to be more specific. After all, you are free to come up with as many blogs as you want. So, if you want to talk about an entirely different topic, then just create another blog for it. When you blog, you should remember that it is also important to be organized.

It is advised that you write a list of things that you want to blog about. Especially if you are just starting out, you might not even have any idea of what to share with the world. Another possible thing that can happen is that you might have too many ideas. Either way, the best advice is to make a list by writing down on paper the potential topics for your blog. If it is your first time making a blog, then focus on creating just a single blog to start. Managing several blogs at the same time can be confusing. Once you have your list ready, which contains different topics, then it is time for you to choose the one that you want to blog about the most. There is really no right and wrong way of doing this. It is more a process of deduction and choosing the one that you really like the most. Do not worry about crossing out those that you think you also like. Remember that this is just the beginning. You can blog about them in the future. For now, your objective is to learn how to create and manage a blog.

Now, some people decide not to blog about their passion or what they are interested in. Instead, they take a more business approach and blog about what is currently *hot* in the market. This way, they know that there is a big and existing market for the topic of their blog. Although there is nothing wrong with this approach, you should not forget that blogging is supposed to be a long-term strategy. How can you enjoy your blog if it talks about something that you are not even interested in? Do not worry; no matter what topic you choose, there is definitely a market for it since your blog has a wide reach — the whole world. Of course, it still cannot be denied that there are topics that have a bigger market than others. For example, a blog about cryptocurrencies these days will definitely attract a bigger number of people, more so than a blog about poetry. Still, there is an existing market for both. So, this would depend on your approach. The good news is that you can surely make money either way you go. This is one of the best things about blogging; you are free to blog about anything you want, and you can still earn a profit from it.

Still, this book strongly suggests that you only blog about something that you are interested in because it is difficult to come up with interesting contents and blog about something that you do not understand and maybe have no interest in.

Get your domain, web hosting, and *WordPress* (self-hosted) platform set up

To come up with a professional blog, you need to get your own domain name. This is also where you get to have your own web hosting in the online world. By doing a search online, you will easily find a list of different sites that seem to offer the same service. Before you choose which site to use to get your own domain name and host your site, be sure to check the latest reviews given on that site. Do not worry; this is easy to do. Simply use your favorite search engine and type the name of the site on the search bar and add the word "reviews." The search engine results pages (SERP) will then show you related pages. One of the most common places to get your own domain name is *Godaddy*. Many people also suggest using *Bluehost*, especially if you are using *WordPress* as your self-hosted site.

Take note that buying your own domain name is actually like renting something online. You will have to pay for it, usually annually, but you can also make advance payments if you want to.

So, why do you need to get your own domain? Well, it is like having your space on the internet that you own. How can you expect people to treat you seriously if you do not even have your own domain or place online? If you are serious about being a blogger, stay away from free blogging platforms that will give you a long and informal domain name. If you use a free platform, you will usually end up with a subdomain like this: *nameofyoursite.blogger.com* or *nameofyoursite.wordpress.com*. Instead of a professional-looking domain name like this: *nameofyoursite.com*.

The problem with using just a subdomain (free domain) is that you have no control over it. It is not your own space online. For example, if you use *WordPress'* free domain, then your whole blog will also disappear if *WordPress* decides to remove that feature, or worse if *WordPress* itself disappears.

Now, it is also important that you choose a good domain name. This is something that you should think about carefully as there is no way that you can change your domain name. For starters, it is advised that you keep it short, simple, and clear. It should also be easy to spell and remember. You do not want to tell it to someone, only to spend so much time explaining to them how to visit your blog online. So, keep it simple, but make it catchy and professional. There are also those who suggest that the name of your blog should also reflect what the blog is about. Now, there are conflicting views on this matter. Some people agree that your blog domain name should reflect what your blog is about, while others do not consider it important, and that it only makes the name longer. So, whether such is a good or bad thing, it is a matter of your own personal preference.

When it comes to choosing your blogging platform, many people suggest that you use *WordPress*. The reason why many professional bloggers suggest *WordPress* is because it is highly customizable and one of the best platforms out there. In fact, it can be said to be the number one blogging platform out there. Even professional writers and authors use the *WordPress* platform for their blogs and websites, and many businesses also use *WordPress* as well. When it comes to blogging, *WordPress* always tops the list. A little bit of drawback with this platform is that you might need a little bit of computer and programming knowledge to use it effectively. Do not worry; there are many free articles and videos online that will teach you how to use *WordPress* to create and structure your blog. If you want a simpler platform, then you might want to try *blogger*. It is the blogging platform of the computer giant, *Google*. However, it should be noted that, what this book recommends, and what many bloggers also recommend, is the *WordPress* platform.

Do not worry, *WordPress* is not really that difficult to use. In fact, if only you could spend a few hours to study it, then you will know just how simple and easy it is. *WordPress* also offers free templates so you can start using your blog right away.

Once you have these things ready, you can now start using and designing your blog. Creating a blog is easy; the challenging part is the design and structure part of it, as well as generate quality content to be posted on your blog on a regular basis.

Set up your blog (blog design, layout, etc.)

So, how do you set up your blog? Well, once you are inside *WordPress*, you can now make certain changes on your blog. You can change the colors, the positionings, add pages, and many others. Thanks to *WordPress'* features that are instinctively easy to understand, you can simply follow the instructions on the platform, and make changes on your own to make the blog more suitable for your needs.

Feel free to design your blog any way you want. Of course, the design will depend on the subject of your blog. See what works for you. After all, it is free to make changes on your blog as many times as you want. Do not rush this process as the design plays an important part that affects the experience of your blog visitors. So, remember to be careful about this matter.

The next thing that you want to take note of is the layout of your blog. It is advised that you pick a simple layout that will make it easy for your blog visitors to navigate the pages with just a click of the mouse.

Another thing to take note of is to divide your blog into different pages. This helps to make your blog more organized. This way, you can have different sections on your blog that will make it easy for your readers to explore.

Since this is a blog, you would want to allow your audience to post comments and interact with throughout. In default mode, commenting is already activated. Now, it should be noted that you have to be careful with answering comments on your blog. Remember to thank your reader for taking time to read and comment on your posts. From time to time, you might encounter some negative comments. If ever this happens to you, just relax and think about it. Who knows, the one who wrote a negative comment might have good intentions and only want you to recognize some mistakes in your posting. So, when you receive a negative comment, give some time to consider and think about it. If you realize that it was made in good faith without any malice, then you should even thank the person who wrote it and be sure to make changes to further improve your blog.

Setting up your blog might take some trial and error. Feel free to make as many changes and modifications as you want. The important thing is to make your blog as functional and presentable as possible.

Post your first content

Once your blog is ready and is already well structured, you can now post your first content. Now, be careful about this.

Remember to only come up with quality contents. A common mistake is to make a well-designed and fully functional blog but end up filling it with poor quality content. Again, ensure that all your blog posts have a good quality. It does not always have to be of high quality, but you should always strive to make every post the best as you can. Focus on the quality.

After creating your first post, then you should follow it up with more quality postings. Your first post is important as your first blog readers/visitors will gauge you by the first thing that they see on your blog. Some people judge a blog too quickly. If they do not like what they see the first time they look at your blog, then they might not take a second look to consider it again, even in the future. This is another reason why you should ensure to only post content that is of good quality. The content on your blog does not always have to be of high quality; a decent quality post will also do. Still, you are encouraged to come up with the highest level of quality that you can.

Before posting your first content on your blog, it is good to have a structured plan on how you want your blog to be. Although a visitor can easily explore the contents of your blog with just a click of the mouse, it is still best if you keep your blog organized. This means that it would be beneficial for you to build the foundation of your blog by laying the basics first. This way, your readers can follow a good flow, much like when reading a book. Of course, this is not always required. After all, there are blogs out there that do not need to have organized content. Now, a common problem is how to organize the sequence of your blog posts once you have already posted them. Normally, in a blog, they are arranged in sequential order with the latest blog post showing first. If you want to rearrange their order, the best way to do this is to change the dates of the blog posts. You can do this by choosing the blog post whose date you want to change and edit the date of post. This might differ depending on the blogging platform that you use, but the important thing is to change the date to reorder the blog posts.

Add more posts

Blogging is a long-term activity. It is also the nature of a blog to be updated with new posts regularly. Hence, you are expected to add more blog posts every now and then. Make sure that every post that you make is of good quality.

Share and engage

Blogging is sharing. Make sure to share your blog with friends. A good way to do this is to use the power of social media. You can also encourage your friends to share your content for you to reach a bigger network. As you blog, you should also engage with your readers. This can be as simple as responding to the comments on your blog.

Pros and cons of free blog platforms

You might be wondering why many bloggers do not encourage using free blog platforms like *Blogger*. There are certain reasons why:

Pros:

Of course, an obvious part of the pros is that such platforms are free to use. You would not have to spend any money at all. Feel free to blog without spending a dime. If you are undecided if you want to be a blogger or not, then you can just start out using a free platform. Since they cost nothing, you are free to make as many blogs as you want without risking any real money. If you are just starting out, especially if you are still undecided whether you should invest in a blog domain, then you might want to start with a free blogging platform and see how it works. It is also easy to convert a free subdomain into a real domain. Yes, you do not have to lose the audience and followers that you have built. This is true if you use *WordPress* or *Blogger*, which is another reason why you should only blog using the best and most famous blogging platforms out there. Free blogging platforms are also an excellent way to test and get a feel for a particular platform before you invest real money into it. Consider it as a kind of free trial.

Cons:

Okay, so what are the cons of using a free blogging platform? Well, since it is free, it is hard to say anything bad about it. However, it is sticking to a free platform that can be a problem. If you just have a subdomain, then you do not have full control and ownership of your space in the internet realm. Free blogging platforms also usually offer only limited features, unlike when you avail from the paid features, and this is understandable. After all, it is all for free, so it is hard to complain about anything.

Why use *WordPress*?

Okay, so why should you use *WordPress*? This is something that many people ask. Is it really that good compared to its competitors? The answer is yes. Whether you want to have a blog or any website, experts suggest that you use *WordPress* because it offers the best and easiest solutions for the needs of your blog. Although it may be more complicated to use than *Blogger*, *WordPress* is more customizable and has a more professional-looking design. Due to its high customizability, you can exercise a lot of control over your blog. Feel free to make changes, even minor changes to the overall look and functionality. With *WordPress*, you can take full control of your blog and make changes and improvements that other platforms could not allow.

As a strong competitor of *WordPress* being *Blogger*, although *Blogger* is much simpler to use, *WordPress* offers more interesting features other than its high customizability. It is also easier to have a store on your blog when you use the *WordPress* platform.

The best way to appreciate the beauty of *WordPress* is by giving it a try. Also, do not be discouraged if people say that you will need some programming knowledge when you use *WordPress*; you do not need to have rich knowledge of programming. Even if you have not read anything about programming, you can still use and take advantage of the *WordPress* platform, but such programming knowledge is a plus. Still, even without any background related to computers, there are many free articles and videos online that you can use to help you customize your *WordPress*-powered blog.

Chapter Three
Make Money with Your Blog

The best ways to make money with your blog

Let us now take a look at the different ways to make money with your blog:

PPC advertising

PPC stands for pay-per-click advertising. This is where you earn money whenever someone clicks on an ad posted on your blog. Another variation of PPC is PPV or pay-per-view advertising. This is where you get to earn money whenever a person views or is able to see the ads on your blog, even if they do not click on it. On average, PPV pays a small portion of a dollar per 1,000 views. If your blog generates lots of traffic, then PPC or any other ad-program can be good for you to earn income.

Now, when you do a search online, you will definitely find different ad programs. Among the different ad programs out there, the one that is strongly suggested by professional bloggers is *Google Adsense Program*. It is the ad program that pays the most, and since it is owned by the tech giant, *Google*, you know that you can depend on it.

The challenge is that *Google* is quite picky with the blogs that they allow to post their ads on. Before you can start having ads appear on your blog, you must first submit your application to *Google*, and it will examine if it would let you post *Google* ads. The problem here is that many bloggers get rejected. But, do not worry; this is not really that hard as long as you know what to do. The key here is to only enroll in the *Google AdSense Program*, and only when you already have an established blog. This means that your blog should have a regular flow of visitors. The traffic does not have to be huge, but it should be decent enough. Make sure that your blog has at least thirty high-quality posts. It is also good if there are active interactions on your blog. This is a good reason to market and share your blog posts on social media and encourage people to share and comment on your works. The more established your blog is, the higher your chances are that *Google* will allow your blog to display its ads.

Another useful tip is to use *GooglePlus*. What is *GooglePlus*? Well, it is the social platform of *Google*. It works just like *Facebook* or *Twitter*. You can connect your blog to *GooglePlus* and share your content with other users on the said social platform. When you use this platform, there is a "plus" symbol. The more pluses you get, the more your content will be recommended to *Google*, which will make it have a higher SEO rating. This will not just increase your chances of being able to display *Google* ads on your blog, but it is also a good way to boost your income by driving more traffic to your blog.

PPC and other similar advertising programs are one of the best ways to earn from your blog. Some people earn more than a regular full-time income simply by posting ads on their blog. However, do not expect to be able to do this quickly as you will still need to establish your blog, and have a regular flow of traffic.

Affiliate Income

Another excellent way to make a profit by blogging is through affiliate links. So, how do you earn affiliate income? This is done by posting something on your blog, usually a review of a product, and providing an affiliate link. If the reader clicks on said affiliate link and purchases the product, then you get a cut from the purchase price. Consider it as if you were an agent selling something, but this time it is made online. There are many affiliate programs online that you can join. The most famous is *Clickbank*. Before you join any affiliate program, be sure to check its reviews online. This is more about promoting a particular product. Some bloggers also come up with comparisons of ads to show the pros and cons between two products. At the same time, they provide affiliate links for both products. The key to earning income from affiliates is by providing helpful and quality content. Do not just rewrite what other blogs have said about the products. It is also good if you can test the products that you are reviewing in person instead of just comparing what other people say about them online.

Remember that you should give value to your readers. Avoid the wrong practice of making the product more attractive than it is. Otherwise, the reader will be misled and end up disappointed. Not to mention, you might end up having bad reviews from your blog visitors. You need to establish a blog that people can trust. Yes, you need people to trust you. If you are working with affiliates, then the best way to do this is to tell the truth about the products that you are promoting or writing about. Do not worry about the products having imperfections or disadvantages. After all, your readers are aware that every product has its disadvantages or cons. The important thing is to tell the truth so that your readers will have the right information. This is how you develop trust in your blog. If you want to be a successful affiliate marketer/blogger, then trust is the number one ingredient to your success. After all, how do you expect someone to click on your affiliate link and make a purchase if he does not even trust you?

Coaching and consulting

If you have knowledge and experience about something, then you might want to offer coaching and/or consulting services on your blog. You can earn as high as you want since you can charge the fee that you prefer. However, just be reasonable and realistic about it. Depending on the subject of coaching that you offer, you can say that the whole world is your potential market. Thanks to technology, you can easily offer your services to countless people just by going online. If you take this approach, it is suggested that you use *LinkedIn*, a social media platform for professionals. This way, you can easily meet professionals who might be interested in what you have to offer.

There is no limit as to the kind of service or coaching that you can offer. There are those who can teach you how to be a better blogger, how to play guitar, how to increase your business income and many other areas of interest. Of course, you cannot expect anyone to hire you as a coach or consultant just out of nowhere. The way to do this is to establish your credentials on your blog. You can do this by posting high-quality content and establish your credibility on the "About Me" page of your blog. Before a person will hire you, you need to earn their trust first.

Membership site

You can also earn money by having a membership site on your blog. The way to do this is to offer some high-quality content for free, and then keep the other content exclusively for paid members. There are many blogs out there that generate a lot of money using this technique. Just be sure to gain the trust of your blog visitors by providing them with free content. People like free stuff because it allows them to test something without risking any money. Just be sure that the quality of those that you offer for free is also good enough to further capture the interest of the market.

You should promote your membership site as you would any other blog. Again, take note that quality remains to be a very important element to your success. You might also want to offer discounts, especially to the first few members of the site, as well as to those who would share your blog on social media. Just like when promoting any other blog or business, you need to spread the word on your blog or business.

Sell eBooks and Other Products (Digital or Physical)

Yes, you can sell on your blog. There are many bloggers out there who make tons of income by offering things for sale on their blog. Since a blog exists in the online world, it is also good to come up with a virtual product, such as an ebook. The best way to do this is to gain as many followers on your blog as you can, and then have an ebook for sale. Indeed, your blog supporters and many other followers would show their support and interest by purchasing your ebook. There are now many ways to sell online. You can use *WordPress*, *PayPal*, third-party services like *Payhip*, and others to handle online transactions. A good thing about selling ebooks is that you can generate as many ebooks as needed at zero cost. The only concern you would have is to come up with a high-quality ebook. There are those who simply put everything from their blog into a book and offer it for sale. This is also possible. If you think of it, since your blog posts talk about the same subject, you can soon compile all of your posts into a book.

Now, the problem is how you can write a book. Some people have no problems with writing a blog post but consider it a big responsibility to come up with a book. Indeed, writing a book is a daunting task. So, what can you do? Well, if you think that your own blog posts cannot make up a whole book, and if you think that you cannot write a decent book on your own, then you can hire a ghostwriter to do the work for you. Of course, in exchange for this special service, you need to pay your ghostwriter a fee. Now, there are no strict rules as to the rate of a ghostwriter. However, a good tip to remember is that you will often get your money's worth. Usually, ghostwriters who would write your book for a few hundred dollars are considered on the low end of the spectrum of ghostwriters. So, do not expect to receive a high-quality work. After all, you cannot expect a real professional writer to write a book for you just for a few hundred dollars. If you want to get a book that is of a professional quality, then you also need to be willing to pay a professional rate. However, it is worth noting that if you get lucky, you might happen to find a talented ghostwriter who would write a decent book for you for a few hundred bucks. Still, do not expect for the work to be of top-notch quality. After all, no real writer would spend more than a hundred hours on your book if he is only paid a few hundred dollars.

The best way to write a book yourself on a subject you are passionate about is to break it up into only writing high quality 1,2 or 3 pages a day. For example, if you only write 2 pages a day, in 150 days or half a year, you will have completed a 300 page book, which is a very good size, many successful books are a lot less in size that that. If you have images and tables included, that 300 could be expanded to maybe 350 pages!

150 days are going to pass you by anyways, how hard can it be to write 2 pages a day? Can you focus 20 minutes a day to do this? If now, how are you going to write your blog posts every day?

You are not limited to just selling books. You can sell anything at all online, including physical objects. The problem with selling material things is that you will have to worry about how you can safely ship the products to your buyer, especially if your buyer resides in a different country. You also have to worry about manufacturing or suppliers, as well as keeping inventory. If you are just starting out, it is strongly suggested that you focus on selling virtual products, like an eBook, to avoid complications.

Blog Promotions

You can also use your blog to promote stuff for a fee. There are bloggers out there who would charge you a fee. In exchange, they will promote your blog, eBook, etc. on your blog. For this purpose, you might want to join *Fiverr*. *Fiverr* is a website where you can offer different gigs. There are people there who earn a nice profit by promoting eBooks on their blog. Of course, you are not limited to just using *Fiverr*. Many other bloggers and authors are looking for sites to promote their blog. If you have a good following and huge traffic, then you can promote your service on your blog. When you do a promotion, avoid overselling whatever it is that you are promoting. Again, you do not want to cheat on your readers. Instead, you want to offer them value by giving them quality information. So, whatever you might promote on your blog, be sure to be honest about it. You should have more loyalty to your blog visitors than the people who ask you to promote their products. After all, if the product that you are promoting is really good, then there is nothing to worry about. Well-established blogs normally charge a premium price for promoting an eBook, or even another blog. You can name whatever price you want, just make it fair and reasonable.

Product Reviews

Another way to make money from your blog is by giving product reviews. Some businesses will be willing to pay you just to post and review their products on your blog. Of course, this does not work for every and all kinds of blogs. Obviously, a business would choose to work with a blog that tackles the same subject as the business. For example, a computer business will most likely hire the service of a person who has a business blog. There are also blogs that specialize solely in giving reviews on different products. This is also the kind of blog that businesses want to pay for. Again, when writing reviews, even though you are paid by the business, it is important for you to be honest.

When reviewing a product, do not just focus on the good side. You should also talk about the disadvantages of the product if any. You can also add some suggestions or tips on how to use the product more effectively.

Sell Your Blog

This is a way to make a huge amount of money with your blog overnight. In fact, you can earn thousands of dollars. However, the consequence is also serious; you will lose your blog permanently. Sites like *Flippa* and *Sedo* are domain marketplaces where you can buy and sell websites, which means that they are also the place where you can sell your blog.

Selling a blog is not easy. Also, buyers look for blogs that are already established. You cannot expect to sell a start-up blog with little following for thousands of dollars, <u>except maybe if you have a really good domain name</u> — however, this is unlikely. If you decide to build and sell blogs for a profit, then this is a good way to go. Just remember that merely listing your blog on such marketplaces is not usually enough. You also need to promote that you are selling your blog. The reason is that there are countless numbers of websites and blogs being sold on such marketplaces so it would be hard to draw any attention to your blog unless you promote it.

Well, as you can see, this is probably the last option that you want to choose to make money from your blog since it also involves losing your blog. However, it is worth it to be included on the list, since this is also a good and effective way to earn a huge amount of money from your blog. Indeed, the price of well-established blogs can go very high.

Chapter Four
Search Engine Optimization

What is SEO?

To have a successful blog, then people should know about it. No matter how many informative articles that you have, it would not do any good if people are not even aware of it. Hence, you need to make your contents discoverable. This is where SEO, which stands for Search Engine Optimization, comes in. You are probably already familiar with this term since it is already very famous online. By optimizing your content for search engines, you can draw more traffic to your blog. This is because proper SEO will place your contents on the first few pages of the search engine results pages (SERP). This means more people will see your postings. If you want to succeed as a blogger, it is a must that you learn about the proper and effective use of SEO.

Optimizing your posts for SEO (use long-tail keywords, quality content, social media, etc.)

Long-tail keywords

When it comes to SEO, perhaps the number one most important tip is to use keywords. Gone are the days when you can just use whatever keywords that come to your mind. Again, the blogging industry has become so much more competitive. Today, what you need is known as long-tail keywords. Long-tail keywords are composed of three or more words that say something about your subject. They are keywords because they are repeated all throughout the article.

You cannot just use whatever keywords that come to your mind. Instead, you should choose long-tail keywords that people search for. You need to be able to know the words that people type in the search bar when they look for something online. So, how do you know the best long-tail keywords to use? Well, many bloggers suggest that you use *Google Keyword Planner*. This planner will allow you to know the number of times a certain keyword or keywords were searched on *Google*. Ultimately, you will know if there is a demand for the keywords that you think of. *Google* will also suggest other keywords that you can use.

But how do you use *Google Keyword Planner*? This planner is quite hard to find if you do not know where to look for it. Here is a little secret: *Google Keyword Planner* is found in *Google AdWords*. Remember from chapter three in the sub-category of PPC advertising; it is *Google's* program that will allow you to post ads and promote your blog. So, the first step is to sign up for a *Google AdWords* account. Once you have an account, then you can find the keyword planner from the *Google AdWords* platform itself.

Do not use a particular keyword just because it has millions of hits. In fact, this may mean that you probably have a keyword that is too broad. It is also not good to be too broad as you will fail to target your real market. Again, the key here is to be as specific as possible. Instead of just searching for *stock market*, you can search for *best stock market strategies 2018*. As you can see, just because a certain keyword has a high number of hits does not necessarily mean that it is the right keyword for you to use.

Many bloggers become dependent on the keyword planner, so some people wonder if it is absolutely necessary to use the said planner. Well, the answer, of course, is in the negative. After all, it is not really that hard to know what people would type in the search bar when they look for something online. The key is to keep it simple and avoid using just one keyword. Again, remember that long-tail keywords are composed of at least three words. Still, if you want to be more accurate and really find out the number of searches for a particular keyword, then the best option you have is to use *Google Keyword Planner*.

Now, avoid the practice known as "keyword stuffing." What is keyword stuffing? It refers to the practice of stuffing your article with your keywords with the hope that it will be more discoverable to search engines. Years ago, this used to work, but it no longer works today. Search engines have already improved, so much so that you cannot expect them to find your blog just by stuffing it with related keywords. Today, what you need to do is provide quality content. You should also maintain your keyword density between two to five percent. There are no hard and fast rules on keyword density or how many times your keywords should appear in every post, but many experts suggest the two to five percent range. It is not recommended to exceed five percent even if you provide high-quality content since the search engine might suspect it to be another form of keyword stuffing.

Quality content

Now, this is a very important part of being a blogger: make sure that you provide your audience with quality content. All the successful blogs out there are those that offer high-quality content. This is actually very common advice, but what does it mean to have quality content? Well, for starters, it means that your posts should contain little to no grammatical and punctuation errors. Needless to say, it also should not have spelling errors. This is as far as the basics are concerned. Now, you should understand that true blog writing means so much more than using correct grammar and punctuation. You should also provide helpful information to your readers. The style of writing is also important. It should not sound so academic that it would bore your readers. At the same time, it should not sound too light that people would find it hard to take you seriously. Being able to come up with quality content may take some practice. However, it should be noted that you do not need to be a professional writer to create quality content. As long as you know what you are writing about, and if it is something that you are interested in, then chances are you can easily come up with quality content. It is also worth mentioning that doing research is an important element of quality writing. Do not forget to cite your sources to avoid plagiarism. Needless to say, stay away from the practice of simply copying and pasting content.

Having quality content is the best way to draw readers to your blog and have them want to share it. In turn, this will drive new traffic to your blog. Make sure that the readers will enjoy reading what you have posted. The only way to do this is to provide them with quality content.

Do not think of this as a complicated process. It is not hard to provide quality content as long as you focus on exposing the facts and share what you know about the subject. Focus on giving quality information. You will soon get used to it to the point that writing quality content will come naturally to you. Again, focus **on the quality of your work.**

Long post

Gone are the days when you can just post a simple 250 or 300-word article and expect for it to generate lots of traffic and followers. Again, the online world is now more competitive than ever. Now, there are still people who think that a 500-word article will be good enough. In fact, many bloggers still think that a 500-word article is the standard length of a good article for purposes of SEO. However, you should know that the internet has changed and evolved significantly. Although 500-word articles are still considered okay, they are no longer considered the best choice if you want to work on your SEO ranking. To improve your site's SEO, it is strongly suggested that you craft longer articles. Although there is still no hard and fast rule as to the most ideal word count to observe, it is suggested that you keep your article somewhere around 1,500-3,000 words. Of course, you also need to make sure that it has high-quality content.

Now, some people find it hard to come up with a long post. It is true that most of the things that you want to share can be summarized in less than 500 words, so how do you reach your desired word count? Just because you want to reach your desired word count does not mean that you should just babble on and play with meaningless words. Avoid talking non-sense. Otherwise, your reader will soon get bored and not read your posts. Instead, what you should do is focus on giving quality information. You can do this by tackling the subject in a very specific way. You can also share your own insights and opinions. Another option you have is to give examples and even suggestions. You can also provide your own analysis of the matter. As you can see, there are many ways to expound on the subject. Once you get used to it, you will see that coming up with 1,500 words, or even 3,000 words, is not such a difficult thing to do.

When you make a long post, it is advised that you also observe the right format and paragraph structure. When writing for an online audience, it is suggested that you avoid using one long paragraph. Instead, you should divide a long paragraph into smaller parts. The reason for this is that there is a difference between reading on a device and reading a traditional printed book. The eyes can get more easily strained when reading on a device. As such, you should help give your readers a more convenient reading experience. A good and easy way of doing this is by observing the right paragraph structure. It is also suggested that you use a simple and decent template to make the reading experience more convenient for your readers.

Use alt text on images

Images can be used to increase your SEO. Take note that it is not the images themselves that will improve your SEO, but the texts that you write — the alt texts. This usually refers to a short line or description that is below an image. You can use this opportunity to mention your keyword and further boost your SEO ranking. It is also worth noting that it is indeed a good idea to include an image, even just a single image, on your posting. Many people find it boring to read a huge block of text. By adding an image, you can make it look more reader-friendly.

Since you will be using images, it is worth noting that you should use quality images that are related to the subject of your posting. You should also use only images that you can legally use. If you are not going to use your own image, then use something that you have permission to post. To be safe, use public domain images. Public domain images are images that can safely be used by anyone, even without the permission of the owner of those images. If you want your image to be unique, then you might want to consider using your own images. There are also premium images that are offered for sale online. Regardless of the image that you use, it is important that you only use images that you have the right to use. Hence, stick to using your own images, public domain images, or images that you have the permission from the owner to use.

Add links

Adding a link can be a good way to direct your reader where to go next. There are two types of links: inbound and outbound. Inbound links direct your reader to another post or article on your blog, while outbound links direct your reader to another post that is located outside of your site. Be sure to add only useful and helpful links. If you use it to promote another post on your blog, then be sure that the said post has a high-quality. This is a good way to encourage your readers to stay and explore your blog further.

Drive more traffic to your blog

The more people that you drive to your blog, the higher your SEO ranking will be. Now, there are many ways to draw traffic to your blog. This is where marketing comes in. Do not worry, we will discuss the different ways to market your blog effectively in the next chapter. If the people who visit your blog like what they read, there is also a good chance that they will share your content with their own network. Just imagine how much traffic this could bring to your blog. In fact, this is how content goes viral on the internet. Therefore, remember to always provide quality content.

Chapter Five
Best Blogging Practices

Writing posts and content

Blogging is mostly about writing posts and content. If you have nothing to write, then you cannot blog. Bloggers are also known for always coming up with new content on a regular basis. Many suggest that you should update your blog with a new content at least once or twice a week.

A good advantage of always updating your blog with new content is that it gets your readers hooked, which ultimately compels them to stay and follow your blog. If a reader knows that you will no longer update your blog, or feels like you would not update it, then it is most likely that they will just ignore your blog or unfollow it. It is worth noting that you should not rush the writing process. A common mistake is to procrastinate. If you are just starting out, you should know that it usually takes time and effort to come up with high-quality content. Make sure to do your research and edit your writing as many times as you might need. Many bloggers try to write content in one sitting. Although this is doable, you should know that most articles that are written in one sitting are usually not that good. Most of the time, they are the articles that are poorly written. Since you are advised to post at least one article a day, this means that you have enough time to do research and to write your article. Do not fall into the pitfall of procrastinating. A good rule of thumb is to never allow a day to pass without adding something to an article draft, be it a line or two, or simply another body of research. The important thing is to always have some sort of development. You might not be used to this kind of discipline in the beginning, but you will surely get used to it after some time. The important thing is to keep on trying, and never stop updating your blog with new and fresh content that your readers will enjoy and find helpful.

It is noteworthy that there are different levels of quality. When you say that something has good quality, that "quality" can still be subdivided. This is because there are many ways of writing and presenting something. Do not worry; over time, your writing skills will improve. Of course, when it comes to improving your writing, the best way to do this is to simply keep on writing. Of course, you are also expected to learn at least the basic skills in writing, such as using proper grammar and punctuation, as well as using correct spelling.

When writing a blog post, make sure to use a catchy introduction. The beginning of your blog post is very important. If it fails to capture the attention of the reader in the first few lines, then chances are the reader will just skip to another article. As a result, they will not be able to read entirely what you have written. Worse, they might not read anything from you after that. To avoid this, make the introductory paragraph of your blog post catchy and interesting so that your reader will be drawn in and want to continue reading. Now, this might take skill to do. The key is to practice writing regularly. Take note that writing is a skill that cannot be taught. Just like any other skill that is worth learning, you need to practice to improve.

Writing high-quality content also depends on your style of writing. Now, there are no hard and fast rules as to the best style of writing to observe. This will most probably depend on your target readership. You should make the flow as smooth and natural as possible. Also, avoid using words that are hard to understand. This is not the time to display the extent of your vocabulary, but rather, to share information with your reader.

Re-purposing news articles strategy

Okay, the truth is that it is not always easy to come up with content to update your blog with. Yes, you may not find any trouble with writing five articles, but once you have been blogging for several months, chances are that you will find it a challenge to come up with new quality content. So, what can you do? Well, there is a practice known as "repurposing content." If you are writing news, then it is referred to as "repurposing news articles." This is not really the best practice, but it is commonly used online. So, how does it work? Simply, it is all about rewriting another person's article or blog post as if it were your own. In the strict sense, this is definitely considered plagiarism, unless you cite the article where you took it from, although, this would be pointless. People who repurpose another person's work do not normally give the credit to whom it is due, as it would be obvious that you only stole the content.

So, how do you do this? Well, you should know that even though the online world is full of plagiarism checkers, they are still very much ineffective. This explains why plagiarism is a common incident online. These days, the use of plagiarism checkers has become popular. However, the problem is that such checkers are not 100% dependable. If a writer knows the secret behind repurposing articles, then these checkers will not be able to detect plagiarism. So, how do you do this? Well, the secret is not to use three consecutive words that are taken directly from an existing work. Following this simple rule will, most of the time, help plagiarism from being detected. You are free to try and see it for yourself.

Now, there is also a good and legitimate way of doing this, and this is what you need to learn. The proper way of doing this is to find a different and unique angle from the article. For example, if the article is about the health benefits of drinking coffee, you might come up with a new article, such as the disadvantages of drinking coffee. When you do this, you do not really copy anything from the article, except maybe a few citations here and there, but the main content will be unique. The key is to use the article only as a guide to lead you to write a different article. This is a proper way of repurposing an article and is not really hard to do. A good piece of advice is to view an article from different angles after reading it. If you practice this enough, repurposing articles will soon be a natural thing for you to do.

Using the *WordPress Yoast* SEO plugin

Before you can use this plugin, you first need to set it up properly and have it installed in your blogging platform. Let us discuss the steps one by one: Once you use *WordPress* as your blogging platform, then you will have access to what is known as *WordPress Yoast* SEO plugin. Simply click on the configuration wizard, and you will be on a guided tour that will assist you in setting up basic settings for SEO. You will be shown a link; click on it, and then you will then be led to the first page of the wizard. Select *configure Yoast SEO*. You will now be taken to the *Environment* page. Except if you are working on a development site, you should select *Option A*. You will now be asked to select a site type, just select *blog*, which is also the first option on the list. The next thing that you need to do is choose if the website represents a company or a person. If you intend to run a personal blog, then click on *Person*. You will now be given an opportunity to connect your social profiles, such as your account on *Facebook, Twitter, Instagram*, other others. With respect to *Post Type Visibility*, it is advised to keep everything *Visible* except the last part which refers to *Post Type Media*. Next, you will be asked if the blog will be managed by multiple authors. Indeed, there are many blogs out there that are run by many authors. However, if you are working on your own, then just select *No*. You will now be led to a page that associates with *Google Search Console*. This page merely refers to how your page or blog ranks when searched in *Google*. It is good to know about this since *Google* remains to be the number one web browser in the world.

You will now be led to the *Title* settings. The title is what will appear in the search result in *Google*. The next thing to do is to wrap up the wizard. You will be asked if you want to sign up for a newsletter and if you want to sing up and use the premium version of the wizard. Take note that you do not need to do any of these. And, voila — you have now set up your *WordPress Yoast* SEO Plugin.

When you use the *Yoast plugin*, you will want to use the metabox. The metabox will let you analyze your content with regard to SEO quality, as well as readability. It will also allow you to configure your settings to help you choose how you want your content to show and function on *Google*, and on your social media channels. Take note that you can easily find the metabox just under the *WordPress* editor.

There is also the *Yoast Analysis* tab. This will allow you to enter a "focus keyword" to help optimize your content. You will want to use some keyword research to find out the best keyword to use. Simply type it into the box and *Yoast* will show you just how optimized it is for SEO. For this purpose, you might want to use *Google Keyword Planner*. You will also find the *Edit Snippet* button which will allow you to edit or change your SEO title and meta description.

There is also the *SEO Analysis* tab. Obviously, the purpose of this is to show you just how optimized your content is for SEO. The *Readability* tab will tell you just how readable your content would be to a human visitor. Again, having high readability is also important, because as a blogger, it is your responsibility to give your blog visitors the best reading experiences.

The *Yoast Social Media* tab will show you just how your content will appear when you share it on social media.

There are many other things that *Yoast* can tell you about your blog. The good thing is that the *Yoast* plugin is mostly intuitive to use so you would not have any problems with it.

Use and Integrate Social Media

The use of social media is very important for a blog nowadays. Although it is not a requirement, it is nonetheless very helpful to the success of a blog. If you think about it, content that goes viral are those that are marketed using social media. In fact, content going viral online only became possible because of social media. This is also an excellent way to draw traffic to your blog.

Social media like *Facebook, Twitter*, and others, are powerful tools that you can tap to spread the word about your blog. Not to mention, countless people love to use social media. For blogging, it is recommended that you use either *Facebook* or *Twitter* being that they are the two biggest and most active social media channels in the world. Of course, you are also free to choose from others.

It is also worth noting that it is not just using social media that matters, but you should also establish yourself on social media. You do this by having a network of quality connections.

You should also integrate social media into the blog itself. The way to do this is by using social media buttons on every blog post. This should allow your blog visitors to conveniently share your content on their own social media channel. You should ensure to make this process fast and east for your blog visitors.

Blogging and social media go hand in hand. Although a blog can still be successful even without any backing from social media, it cannot be denied that it could do much better if only it also makes use of the power of social media.

Now, you need to know how to properly use social media to promote your blog. There are many social media channels out there. Many bloggers suggest that you use *Facebook* and/or *Twitter*. If you just want to use a single social media channel, then many agree that the number one social media channel in the world is *Facebook*, so it's a good idea to promote your blog on this channel. You are also free to use other social media channels but take note that *Facebook* and *Twitter* are the primary channels that you want to be into.

Being involved in social media channels is one thing, but effectively using them to promote your blog is another. However, the problem here is that many people do not know how to use social media to draw traffic to their blog. There are certain points that you need to know:

Timing

You should observe proper timing at all times. Although this is something simple, the sad truth is that many people lose their followers by posting too many times in a single day. Remember not to bombard your followers with too many posts. Instead, what you should do is identify the best time to post online. To do this, you may have to make a few trial-and-error runs. A good way to do this is by posting at different times of the day or night, and then identify the best time when most of your connections are active online. This is to ensure that they will be able to view your posts. Many expert bloggers also advise that you should stick to only three to five posts a day. Again, it is not good to bombard your followers with so many blog posts, so choose your posts wisely.

Keep it simple

Keep your posting simple. A good rule is to simply introduce what the blog post is about using a few lines or sentences, and then add a link that will lead your viewer to the blog post. You should also add an attractive image to compel people to look. Studies show that more people will take the time and effort to read your content if they are accompanied by an interesting image. This is true, especially on social media. As the saying goes, "A picture is worth a thousand words." Use the power of images to your advantage.

Take a break

Building a profitable and successful blog takes time. You should give your blog a few months, at least four months to up to a year, before you can see a significant amount of profits rolling in. Of course, if you are lucky, then you might earn a huge amount of income even within the first week, especially if you have a huge following. People usually hit a quick success by selling a high-quality eBook on their blog. But, in the real world, although such quick gains are possible, there is a higher probability that you will not earn anything in the first month. Use that time for building a foundation. It is wrong to advise beginners to focus on profits right away. The first few months of blogging should be focused on building a good foundation, which includes establishing a reader base, and quality connections or followers.

Regardless of whether you have a new blog or a blog that is already established in its niche, you should learn to take a break from time to time. You should view a blog as an investment and not a quick way to make money. It is also common for new blogs to not get enough exposure. Hence, it is normal for high-quality articles only, to get a good number of readers months after it is published. Building a blog empire takes time, just as building a good number of active followers on social media. This is because, apart from producing high-quality content, you also need to build good relationships. Again, you need to build trust. These things are not easy to make, and they always take time. Therefore, take a break from time to time, and do not rush the development of your blog. Do not forget that by allowing yourself to rest, you will be able to blog more effectively.

Catchy message

When you blog, you get to communicate something to your readers. If you want your blog visitors to be interested in your blog, then you should deliver an interesting message. **If your content fails to satisfy the interest of your readers, then chances are they will just move on to another blog and forget about yours.** The worst part is that they will probably never visit your blog ever again, especially if they did not like what they read the first time they visited it. The Web has grown so much that you have to really stick out, focus in on really off-the-wall articles or video posts, try to focus on a sub niche within a niche!

Now, there are no hard and fast rules on what it takes for a message to be catchy. Still, the number one advice is to provide your readers with high-quality information. Another important thing to focus on is to relay that information in an easy to understand manner. This means that you should be able to express your thoughts in writing, effectively. Now, this might take some practice, especially if writing is not your strong point, but it is nonetheless learnable. Just keep on writing, and you will surely improve. Do not worry; bloggers do not need to be professional writers, although, it helps if you can develop your writing skills to that of a professional. If you just take the time to notice it, you will see that many bloggers write in a natural manner as if they were just talking to you. Now, be careful about this. Coming up with a good content that has a natural and smooth flow, does not mean that you do not have to think about the words as you write them down. Rather, it is all about being able to communicate effectively through your writing.

Imagery is Important

It can be intimidating to be welcomed to a new blog that has nothing in it but huge chunks or blocks of texts. It is also suggested that you add an image or even several images to make every post more presentable. Needless to say, you should use an image that is relevant to the subject that you are discussing in your post. Also, do not forget to use *alt text* on images to help increase your SEO ranking.

Quality

Of course, when it comes to blogging, quality is the number one most important thing to take note of. It is the quality of your work that will give it value. The problem is that there are bloggers who do not spend enough time crafting their content.

Take note that professional bloggers usually spend hours, or even a few days, to produce a single article to post on their blog. This is how important quality is. Do not worry; once you are finished creating a post, it will be on your blog forever. So, you might as well give every post on your blog your very best. Make sure to provide your readers with important and helpful information. You should also deliver your message in a concise and interesting manner. In everything that you do on your blog, always put quality as your priority.

Quality is a very important element in any successful blog. You can take a look at the notable examples of successful blogs in this book, and you will notice that they all possess excellent quality. In the same way, if you want your blog to be successful, make sure that you fill it with high-quality content.

Never plagiarize

Plagiarism is rampant online. Many bloggers engage in rewriting other people's content. Take note that *Google* does not like duplicate content, and duplicate content does not just mean articles that are written in the same words, but also to those articles that say the same things, even if it's written using different words. If you want to have a successful blog, then it is important for you to focus on uniqueness.

It is unfortunate that some people think that since a particular article has passed *Copyscape* or other plagiarism checkers online, it already means that the article is free from plagiarism. This is not correct. Take note that plagiarism includes any act where you claim another person's idea as your own. Hence, even if your article is written using different words and passes *Copyscape*, it does not always mean that it is already free of plagiarism.

To avoid plagiarism, you should learn to cite your sources and references. To do this, you can follow the APA or MLA formatting. There are many websites online that will teach you how to use such formatting. However, if you find the instructions difficult to follow, you can just use your own way of citing your references. Just be sure to cite all your sources, and do not claim them as your own.

Of course, the best way to avoid plagiarism is by sharing your own unique ideas. Be sure that when you cite something that is not common knowledge or comes from another person, always cite your source clearly. Also, although it is good to use *Copyscape* or any other plagiarism checker, it is not good to rely on them completely.

Engage

You should engage with your blog readers. The way to do this is to enable comments on your blog to allow your readers to react to your post. Be sure to respond to every comment, and always respond nicely even if you are given a negative comment. The more you engage with your readers, the more they will feel connected to you on a personal level. It is also fine to use this if you write under a pen name. The important thing is to have a space for interaction with your blog visitors and readers. By having a conversation with your readers no matter how brief, you are able to form a good relationship that will make them want to come back to your blog.

Now, the problem is that bloggers fail to produce content that is worth commenting on. The number one rule is to offer high-quality content. The next thing that you want to do is share rich insights that will make the reader think or ask a question. Another thing you can do is to be the one to ask the question and politely tell your readers to place their answers or thoughts in the comments box. Still, the number one requirement is for you to provide high-quality content. If you do not provide your readers with quality content, then you cannot expect them to take the time and effort to even engage and comment on your blog post.

Engaging with your readers and followers is a normal part of being a blogger. This is something that you will do on a regular basis. Now, this engagement should not be limited to your blog. You should also engage with the content of others, especially with other bloggers.

Call to action

It is worth noting that most people who search for answers online are open to suggestions. In fact, this is obvious since the reason why they look for blogs or websites online is to learn the opinions of other people. This makes them more open to suggestions, which is something that you should take advantage of. Therefore, do not forget to include a "call to action" message. A call to action message is a message that suggests to your readers what to do next.

A call to action message is usually placed right after the article. The reason for this is that you first need to convince your reader to listen to you. To do that, they must first read and like your high-quality article. Now, right after reading your article, you can then insert your call to action message. Remember to keep your message short and simple. It is a good practice to limit it to just one or two sentences. Of course, you should use a hyperlink to lead your reader to the next action.

It is helpful to use a call to action message to offer a product or service to your readers. It can also be a way to suggest another page on your site that you think would be helpful to your reader. In an article, it is common to use even up to three inbound links. However, sometimes you need to guide your readers as to the best article that they should read next. For example, if your article is about making money with advertisements posted on your blog, then a call to action to read your article about *Google Adsense* may be the best suggestion that you can make. Having a call to action message is one of the best things that you should have on your blog. Use it wisely.

How do you use a call to action message properly? It is true that many people are aware of this technique, but not everyone knows how to apply it properly. For starters, you should know that you should only use a call to action after you gain the trust of your readers. How can you expect the readers to do as you say if they do not even trust you yet? So, the first step is to make the readers trust you. As you may already know, the way to do this is to provide them with high-quality content for free. As long as they see your posts to be something useful and helpful to them, the more trust you will gain.

Examples of successful blog sites

To give you more inspiration, let us look at some notable blogs throughout the world:

> ➤ Huffington Post

This only started in 2015. Today, it has monthly visitors of more than 110 million. Not only that, it has a monthly revenue of around fourteen million dollars. It was originally called *Huffington Post* but has been renamed simply, *HuffPost*.

> ➢ Mashable

Mashable started in 2005. It now has monthly visitors of around 24 million. Its estimated revenue per month is around two million. *Mashable* was founded by Pete Cashmore, and it focuses on tech news and social media. In today's world, these two fields are considered hot topics.

> ➢ NerdFitness

This blog has more than 50,000 subscribers and makes an income from product sales. Although its revenue appears to be private, there is no doubt that it is one of the most successful blogs out there with more than 50,000 subscribers. If you are into fitness and exercise, then this is the go-to blog for you. Better yet, why not start a blog of your own just like *NerdFitness*?

> ➢ Smashing Magazine

This blog was founded by Sven Lennartz and Vitaly Friedman in 2006. To date, it earns around $215,000 every month. It makes revenue by offering tutorials on how to make money for those who are into web design and development fields. It uses a membership area where paid members can learn from various tutorials on how to make money. Judging by the status of this blog, it can be said that the founders know what they are talking about as they are one of the most notable and successful blogs on the list.

> ➢ Lifehacker

If you are fond of surfing the web, then you are definitely familiar with *Lifehacker*. This blog was founded in 2005. Its monthly revenue remains unknown, but it has more than 23 million monthly visitors, so just imagine how much this blog is earning. As the name implies, this blog shares tips and tricks on how to get things done. This is a really interesting site. If you have not seen it yet, then you should definitely take a look.

➢ Perez Hilton

This blog started in 2005. It is a blog that spreads gossip and scandals of celebrities with a personal commentary from Perez himself. Although, not at the top of the blogging industry, it has a monthly revenue of around $575,000. It has more than 14,500 monthly visitors.

➢ Gizmodo

Gizmodo is a blog about design and technology. It was founded in 2002, and now has a monthly revenue of around $325,000. At the same time, it also contributes in the areas of science and politics. It quickly rose to popularity and makes income through paid advertising on its site. It also positions its ads strategically on the page to avoid giving its visitors any inconvenient experience.

➢ Art of Manliness

This is another famous blog throughout the world. The title of the blog says it all. It deals with things that matter to men. This blog uses long and in-depth articles to educate its readers. It makes its income from ads, affiliate links, and product sales. Although its monthly revenues remain unknown, it has around 150,000 subscribers.

There are many other blogs out there that make lots of money.

Indeed, some people have left their office jobs and make a living from the comfort of their home, blogging about the things that they love and are personally interested in. Although creating a well-established blog can be a long and arduous journey, it is definitely one of the best options that you can take.

Choose popular blog topics and niches

If you want to blog for money, then you can simply focus on popular blog topics and niches. After all, even though you can exercise passion when you blog, if earning money is your main objective, then you might as well think objectively to increase your chances of success. For example, if all other things being equal, you can expect to generate more traffic with a tech blog than a blog about poetry. Of course, this does not mean that there are no chances to succeed at blogging about poetry or other "minor" topics, but it will be much more challenging. Hence, if money is your main objective for blogging, then you should approach blogging as a business. A good way to do this is to come up with a marketable product. In this case, it is whatever the topic your blog will be.

Now, the blogging industry has become much more competitive. Although you can focus on discussing a broad topic, many suggest that you should choose a niche. A niche is a much more specific subject of your topic. For example, if you want to have a business blog, what exactly about business do you want to focus on? Is it about doing business with China, or is it about making money by investing in cryptocurrencies? It is best to be as specific as possible, but do not make it very limiting to the point that you cannot write many details about it. Remember that blogging is a long-term journey, so be sure to pick a topic that you can discuss in detail for a long time.

So, how do you know what topics are popular? Well, a good way to figure this out is to be more observant of the news. What are the latest trends? You can also stick to topics that have a sure market such as technology, fashion, and business. You simply have to identify your niche in each topic. The niche is a specific subject where you want to specialize in by discussing it at length. Another good piece of advice is to study what is trending on social media. This way, you will have an idea of the topics that are considered hot and those that you should avoid. Now, be cautious of falling into the pitfall of choosing a niche that only lasts for a short time in popularity. You should also consider the behavior of the market, which is composed of people whose minds and preferences often change over time. Take as much time as you need to learn more about the market before you start blogging. Remember that blogging is a long-term journey so make your decisions carefully.

It is also not a good idea to just follow the trend. Take note that there are many other bloggers out there. Before you venture into creating a blog, you should also consider the level of competition. Is there anything that you can offer to the market to differentiate your blog from the others and give value to the market? If your blog does not offer any new value, then chances are it will be very difficult to be established in the market.

Quality over quantity

Be sure to focus on the quality of your work. However, take note that this does not mean that quantity is no longer important. Although, many will tell you to focus on the quality, take note that you should also focus on the quantity. Both elements are important. You cannot just drop one or ignore the other. But, what is a quality piece of work? There are no hard and fast rules on this matter. However, it can be said that a work is of high-quality if it is able to do well with what you had intended for it. For example, if you write an article about the benefits of drinking green tea, then you can say that it is good enough if your readers learn from it. This will depend on the information that you share. Be sure to back it up with solid research, and do not forget to cite your sources, if any.

Both quality and quantity are important. Do not listen to those who just say that it is only quality that is important. In the internet age, quantity is also important as it increases your discoverability. However, it is also worthy to note that the quality of your work is also important. Hence, focus on both at the same time.

Avoid the practice of combining good and bad quality content on your blog. Remember that it is better for you not to post any content at all in a week, instead of posting something that has poor quality.

With respect to quantity, there is no strict rule as to how many posts you should have on your blog. However, it is suggested that you should post at least one new content on your blog every week.

Connect with other bloggers

You might think that bloggers who also write about your subject are nothing more than your competitors. This is not actually the case. In fact, it is even common for bloggers to help promote one another's blogs. You should keep in mind that in the online world, you will get the same treatment as you would treat others. If you connect with other bloggers and help them promote their content, there is also a good chance that they will do the same for you. There is also a great deal that you can learn simply by observing other bloggers. Unlike other businesses or investments where you will have to worry about your competitors, you would not have to face the same issues when you engage in blogging. On the contrary, your "competitors" might even help promote and bring new traffic to your blog. It is also much easier to connect with other bloggers these days since there are many online groups and forums that you can participate in.

Do not wait for other bloggers to connect to you. Instead, you should take the initiative and be the one to connect with them. There are many ways to do this. A simple way is by commenting on their posts. Another thing that you can do is simply connect with them on social media. You can also like and/or share their content. As you can see, you can do all of these in the comfort of your home; you simply have to be sure to take the time to do it.

Try to build a positive relationship with other bloggers and learn as much as you can from them. It is considered common online practice for bloggers to help promote each other's posts. This is probably how blogging differs from a traditional business. When you are a blogger, you get to develop a sense of mutual relationship with other bloggers, including those who belong to your niche.

When you socialize online, take note of the rule that you will most likely be treated in the same way that you treat others. Hence, the golden rule, "Do unto others as you would have them do unto you." If you comment on other people's works, then there is a good chance that they will also comment back on your post. This is like the ethics of social media. Now, from time to time, you might encounter negative or even offending comments on your posts. When this happens, it can definitely catch you off guard and would want to make you just lash out at the person who wrote it. But, remember to just relax if ever this happens to you. The best response would be to take it easy and relax. Do not allow yourself to be affected. Now, once you know that you are relaxed enough that you can control yourself, then you can now examine the comment. Was it made just to hurl an insult at you, or does it make a good point after all? If the said bad comment is baseless, then you can either reply politely or simply ignore it. If the comment has a good point, then you can even thank the one who wrote the comment for taking the time and effort to suggest improvements on your blog. Pay attention to constructive criticisms on your blog and make adjustments when possible to further improve the overall quality of your blog.

Marketing

If you want to have a successful blog, then know that marketing plays a very important role. In fact, if you do not market your blog, then there is only a slim chance that it will ever be successful. After all, how will people know about your blog if they do not even know that it exists?

As you may already know, when it comes to marketing, the use of social media is the primary key. By sharing your posts with your connections, there is a good chance that they will also share it with their own network, and this is actually how content on the internet goes viral.

Marketing is the quickest way to spread the word about your blog and draw traffic to it. However, avoid overmarketing your blog. A common mistake is to spend more time with marketing than in creating quality content.

Take note that before you market your blog, be sure that there is something worth marketing about. Remember that no matter how good your marketing is, it will not do any good if the product or blog itself is not valuable enough. Marketing will only make people take notice of what you want to show them. It is still the blog itself that has to provide value to its readers/visitors.

Google AdWords

One of the best ways to draw traffic to your blog is by using *Google Adwords*. This is a *Google* program that will allow you to display ads on websites. Instead of displaying *AdSense* ads on your blog, it is you who is going to post your ads on other people's sites, including the *Google* search pages. Do not worry; this is easy to do. The only drawback is that it is not a free service. The good news is that it is very cheap and costs less than twenty dollars to do. Just go to the *Google Adwords* website, sign up, and then you simply fill in the details of a simple process, and then you can have your ads posted on different sites, including *Google* partner sites if you want. You can also target the places where you want your ads to appear. In fact, you can even target it in such a way that your ads will only appear in selected cities.

You can also choose the keywords when your ads will appear. Make sure to use targeted keywords to avoid wasting your money. You can use the *Google Keyword Planner* which is already included in the *Adwords* platform to identify the best keywords to use. Take note that just because a certain keyword phrase has millions of searches a month, it does not mean that it is already a good keyword to use. You should make sure that it is not composed of generic words but express clearly what your blog is about.

Another interesting feature of *Google Adwords* is that you will definitely get your money's worth. This is because you will only be charged a fee every time your ad gets an actual click. If people just see your ad displayed, then you would not have to pay anything. You can also set the maximum amount that you are willing to pay per click on your ad.

Indeed, the use of *Google Adwords* is one of the best and easiest ways to draw traffic to your blog. The good news is that it is very affordable and highly effective. This is definitely something that you should give a try. Even when your blog is still young with a low SEO rate, you can use *Adwords* to draw traffic to your blog. Once you are able to establish your blog, then chances are that you will no longer have to use *AdWords*. However, if you are promoting a service, then you will definitely find *AdWords* to be very helpful.

Join *GooglePlus*

Although not a requirement, you may find that joining and participating in *GooglePlus* is an excellent way to draw traffic to your blog. *GooglePlus* has many communities for various topics. It also has many active users. By joining the right community that is related to your blog, you can easily meet people who are interested in the topic of your blog. The good thing here is that once they share your content with the people in their network, then you can reach a bigger market. It is also worth noting that most people on *GooglePlus* are very supportive. So, if you are looking to build good relationships and establish a regular stream of traffic, then this is a social media platform that you should try.

Guest post

Guest posting is another effective way to drive traffic to your blog. But, what is guest posting? Guest posting simply means posting an article on another person's blog or website. You also get to keep the by-line, so people will know that you are the author of the article. You might be wondering then: how can guest posting help you promote your blog? Most blogs that accept guest posts will allow you to include a short bio and a link to your site. This is how you promote your site. And, what is more, most established blogs pay for guest posts. Hence, not only will you be able to promote your blog, but you can also earn money at the same time. It is not uncommon to find blogs that pay more than fifty dollars for a 500-word article guest post.

Take note that you should aim to guest post on well-established blogs. These blogs have a huge following. Just imagine how much you can benefit if you are able to lead the traffic from that blog to your own. However, to make those people take an interest in checking out your blog, you need to provide them with an interesting and useful article. If you do, then they may be persuaded to find out more about you — and that is by checking out the link that leads to your blog.

It should also be noted that well-established blogs do not accept just any kind of guest post. Normally, you will have to pass the editorial guidelines, and you need to come up with a high-quality article. This usually takes a good level of writing skills. Do not worry, if the blog where you intend to guest post does not accept your article, you can just publish it on your own blog. If you really want to guest post and promote your blog, and the only hindrance is that you cannot write effectively, then maybe this is when you should consider hiring a professional ghostwriter.

How will you know if a blog accepts guest posts? Most of these blogs or sites provide a "Write for Us" page or editorial guidelines on their blog. Also, if you notice that a particular blog has many authors, then it may be a sign that it accepts guest posts. The best way to find out is to contact the blog's admin via the "Contact Us" page. You can also do a search online for a list of blogs and websites that accept guest posting. Just be prepared to write a compelling query letter and a high-quality article.

Find your voice

You should find your blogging voice. Since blogging is mostly about writing, then this is the same as your writing voice. Now, this is not that easy to find. However, it is important for you to find it, not only to write more powerfully and truthfully, but also to differentiate yourself from the rest. This voice has something to do with how you write and express yourself. If you are just starting out, it is good to learn from the works of the masters. However, a natural tendency is to copy them, as well as how they write. Although this is good if you are just a beginner, you should know that it is wrong to make yourself write like someone else. Instead, what you should do is to use the voice of the masters as a guide to help you find your own writing voice. Write in a way that is most natural to you. There is no hard and fast rule on how you can find your voice. However, as you mature as a writer/blogger, then you will be able to find it. This is where you write just the way you write and not to sound like somebody else. This refers to the real you. Although this is more important in creative writing, it is also a strength when you write a blog.

Now, even if you already know your voice, you should be careful about not exercising it correctly. Remember that blogging is still different from creative writing, so avoid using complicated phrases and sentences. The important thing to keep in mind is to be you.

Establish a good relationship with your readers

This is probably one of the best ways to have a successful blog. Yes, you should create and maintain a good relationship with your blog readers, especially those who visit your blog regularly. When the author of the *Harry Potter* series wrote a different book under a pen name, the book did not do very well in the market. However, when the people learned that the author of that book was also the author of *Harry Potter*, the book significantly increased in sales. As you can see, it is not just what the market thinks about your work that matters. Another thing that is important is what the market thinks of you and if the people like you.

So, how do you establish a good relationship with your readers? Well, the first requirement is for you to provide them with high-quality content. This is how you can make the readers happy. If they do not like what they read on your blog, then you cannot expect for them to visit your blog again. Hence, always keep in mind that the quality of your work is very important. You do not need to be a professional writer to start a blog, but at least make sure to give your readers helpful information.

Establishing a good relationship with your readers should become a regular practice. It is not something that you do for a day and forget about the next day. Now, it should also be noted that establishing a good relationship is a process. This is why you cannot just ignore it. Instead, turn it into a habit. If you come to think of it, it is not really that difficult at all. It is just a matter of observing the best blogging practices that every serious blogger should do.

After giving your readers helpful content, you should give them a chance to get in touch with you. A good way to do this is to allow comments to be posted on your blog, per post. You can also add a contact page where people can send you a private message at any time. Needless to say, you should take as much time as you need to respond to the comments. Appreciate the fact that a person took the time and effort to comment on your blog, not to mention they also read your post before even commenting, so it is only right and just to give them some of your time and write a kind reply. Be sure to observe decency at all times, even when responding to a negative comment. As the saying goes, "Always be professional, not because the other person is, but because you are."

Establishing a good relationship with your readers is an excellent way to draw even more traffic to your blog as your readers will also be the one to help you spread the word about your blog. What is more, since you treat them nicely, they will probably say nice things about your blog, and this is a good way to draw more people to it.

Are Blogs The Way To Go?

Blogging is definitely a proven way to make money online. By now, you already have the basic knowledge you need to create a blog and start your journey to making money with it. Although there is no guarantee that you can make a nice profit in five months, there is a good chance that if you apply the teachings in this book, you can effectively monetize your blog.

Keep up to date on trends – for example; video blogging is becoig extremey popular and effective. People are so distracted nowadays that they have little time to READ content and would rather just watch a video.

YouTube has become the #2 search engine in the world and if you create and link your video posts to you blogging website domain, this is highly favored by Google, which will probably help your SEO score. Obviously Google wants to keep all the traffic in their own network, so this only helps you.

Another opportunity right now in 2018 is placing cheap YouTube video ads. This is a great way to get traffic to your blog if you have the budget. There is plenty of online articles and videos on how to set up and start a low budget YouTube video advertising campaign in Google.

Monitor what other successful bloggers are doing, if you notice, most are simply acting as a media company, sort of like a news channel in a way.

Do not rush the learning and the development process. Blogging is learnable and becoming more complex every year, but you need to be committed to it. This means that you should spend time and effort to develop your blog. If you do well, then there is a good chance that your blog will pave the way towards financial freedom. Is this possible? As you already know, the answer is a resounding yes. In fact, there are so many people out there who have left their usual office job and now make a full-time income blogging in the comfort of their home. The good news is that you can do it, too. However, you need to give yourself a chance to do it, and you need to give it focus and dedication to make it work.

The next step is to apply everything that you have learned about blogging and use that knowledge to turn your blog into a goldmine of profits, it's already been done by thousands of other bloggers worldwide.

Getting To Five Figures a Month In Blogging

Certainly a very achievable goal but will require patience and persistence like ANY OTHER BUSINESS today.

The easiest way to show you the multitudes of strategies and angles you can approach to get to five figures per month in five months is for you to visit the following website/blogs where there is a wealth of information and articles that has everything you need to get started right now

- https://www.smartpassiveincome.com
- https://nataliebacon.com/blog-income-reports
- https://www.makingsenseofcents.com/category/business-income
- https://www.melyssagriffin.com/topics/income-report/
- https://nataliebacon.com/income-report-2017/

(the last link/blogger has tons of good resources for beginning bloggers)

The Best Wordpress Webhosting Service

www.Internetweb.Host

- Full cPanel license and add on software's

- FREE website and cyber security

- Solid state srives

- Fast loading times

- Free DNS management

- 100 add on domains per account

- Unlimited emails

- Free Wordpress installation

Book Two

WordPress For Beginners

"How to Quickly Set Up Your Own Self Hosted WordPress Site and Domain for Beginners - All For Under $25.

Plus Real World Tips & Tricks To Save You Time & Energy"

Updated For 2019

Lee Sebastian

Published By:
Positive Impact
PositiveImpactBooks.com
Cleveland, Ohio

Table of Contents

Chapter One

WordPress 101: The Wonders of WordPress

WordPress is a web software that you can use to create your website or blog. It was written in PHP programming language. Since it was released in 2003, it became one of the most popular web publishing platforms. Today, it supports more than seventy million websites and growing.

But, what a lot of people don't know about Wordpress is that it is more than just a blogging tool. It is also a flexible and powerful content management system or CMS. It allows you to build and manage your own website using your web browser! It is powerful, easy to use, and most of all – it's an open source project. This means that it's free because hundreds (if not thousands) of volunteers all over the world are constantly improving its code.

WordPress allows people to build a website without writing a single code. It is open source, this means that the code behind the software is available and openly shared with whoever who wants to improve it. It is supported, maintained, and developed by a community and not by a company.

Benefits of WordPress

Even if WordPress was created a decade ago, developers are still raving about it. And to be honest, nothing comes close to it. Here's a list of the top benefits of using WordPress as your content management system (CMS) software:

WordPress has polished features.

WordPress is definitely one of the best content management and website builder platforms. It has polished features that allow you to create a personal blog or website in just a few minutes.

1. It is easy to use.
You do not have to be a seasoned programmer to use WordPress. If you know how to use a computer and run any Microsoft office program, you can create a website using WordPress.

WordPress allows you to launch a professional website quickly without coding. In fact, you can launch a website in just a matter of hours. If you want to get into the web design business, WordPress is a great place to start.

2. It has an extensive functionality.
It has a wide plugin directory which we will discuss later on. This allows you to easily, quickly, and inexpensively add functionality to your website. If there's any feature that you want to add to your website, there's a way to do that without coding or spending money. You can add a calendar or sell digital products, you can simply add that feature to your WordPress website.

3 It is FREE.
If you're a small business owner, you would want to save money and take advantage of anything that's free. WordPress is a powerful website builder and content management system that's free. You do not have to pay for anything out of pocket. You just have to pay for the domain name and hosting.

4 It is flexible.

You do not have to wait for your web developer. WordPress allows you to make changes to your website yourself. Since you don't have to wait for a few days for your web designer to make the changes, you can quickly alter the content of your website.

5 It is SEO-friendly.

Your website is no good unless it is visible in the search engine results page of Google or Yahoo. SEO or search engine optimization is a process of making your website visible on the search engine results page by targeting specific keywords. Now, this concept is too complex or intimidating for small business owners.

WordPress takes a lot of the complexity of SEO and makes sure that all your website pages are set up in a way that your potential clients will easily find you on Yahoo, Google, or MSN.

6 WordPress allows you to add multiple users.

As the administrator of a WordPress site, you can add multiple users to help manage your site.

7 It allows you to create mobile-friendly website.

You do not have to create a second website for mobile users. WordPress automatically recognizes if a website visitor is using a mobile device or a web browser.

8 It allows you to manage your time.

WordPress allows you to add multiple posts and schedule them to publish on your website over a twelve week period. This allows you to manage your time well.

9 It allows you to connect your website content to your social media account.

WordPress automatically integrates your blog posts to your Twitter, Facebook, and even, LinkedIn account.

10 You'll have a fast learning curve.

Here's what's awesome about WordPress — it's easier to use than Microsoft Word. You can learn how to post new pages, edit content, and add photos in just a few hours. You can learn how to use WordPress by watching YouTube tutorials.

11 It is secure.

Many people think that WordPress is not secure, because it is an open-source software. But, the opposite is true. This content management system is secure because of the diligent efforts of the members of the WordPress community. Hundreds, if not thousands, of programmers are working to improve its security each day. This is the reason why WordPress has endured a number of high profile attacks over the past few years.

12 It allows continued readership.

WordPress is so easy to use that it encourages you to post content regularly. This encourages web users to repeatedly visit your site. WordPress automatically integrates RSS feeds — a software that increases your readership.

RSS stands for Really Simple Syndication. It is a way for blog readers to track the content of different websites in one news aggregator. The biggest benefit of RSS is continued readership. It allows readers to continue reading your content without visiting your website.

To access your RSS feeds, you just need to go to www.yourdomainname.com/feed.

13 It is popular.

WordPress runs on more than 60% of self-hosted websites. It is massive, huge, and reliable.

Core Features

It is not an exaggerating to say that WordPress is like the Holy Grail of web development. Programmers and web developers around the world love WordPress because of its amazing features which include:

Application Framework

WordPress can help you build apps, too. It has a number of features that you can use to build apps like HTTP requests, user management, translations, databases, and URL routing.

Custom Content Types

WordPress has a number of default content types. But, it is also flexible as it allows you to create metadata, taxonomies, and custom post types.

Theme System

WordPress is known for its theme system. The WordPress application program interface (API) helps to create both simple and complex themes.

WordPress themes are innately multipurpose so you can use for multiple websites. You can use a single theme for different platforms, so it allows you to save money. The theme system comes with a demo and they are packed with "ready to use" shortcodes. This means that you can create a theme even if you do not know how to code. You can even use this system to create eCommerce codes.

The Latest Library

WordPress has a library filled with useful scripts such as Backbone.js, jQuery, Plupload, and Underscore.js.

Plug in System

What's amazing about WordPress is that it has a plug in system. This means that you can add certain functionalities to your WordPress website.

Wordpress plugins are also written in PHP programming language and they can be integrated seamlessly into your website.

Wordpress has a powerful but easy to use system that allows you to install and uninstall plugins from the admin area of your website. You can also download and manually install the plugins using FTP client.

There are thousands of Wordpress plugins. In fact, you can add plugins for many uses like social media, galleries, images, security, and SEO. We will discuss the more popular ones in the later part of this book.

Wordpress websites are easy to build and manage. Anyone who can use Microsoft Word can build a WP website. It is portable which means that you can use it from any type of computer and it is SEO friendly, too. This means that WP websites have the ability to perform better in various search engines like Google or Yahoo.

It also helps to save time and money. Let's face it, dealing with a web developer is challenging and often frustrating. If you use WordPress, you can build and manage your site yourself, so you do not have to hire a web developer. You also do not have to waste time communicating to your web developer to request for site changes.

Most of all, WordPress has an awesome blog feature that's easy to use and maintain. WordPress is a powerful tool that you can use to create and manage website.

Chapter Two

What is PHP?
(Static HTML Websites vs PHP-Based Websites)

As mentioned earlier, WordPress is a PHP website. It is an acronym for Hypertext PreProcessor. It is the most commonly used open source scripting language and it can be embedded into HTML. It allows you to create scripts and web pages.

PHP is a server-side scripting language that was developed in 1995. This means that the code is executed on the server side and not on the client side. It allows you to create web pages that are NOT static.

Before we discuss PHP and differentiate it from HTML, let's discuss what HTML is. Well, HTML is the acronym of HyperText Markup Language. It is the backbone and the structure of a website. It is one of the core components of the internet along with other front-end machineries such as JavaScript and CSS. It is technically a set of symbols and characters that tells the internet how to display a page's text or image. Each markup code is called an element, but it's popularly known as a "tag".

Here's a list of common HTML tags:

<body> - Defines the body of the text

<h1> to <h6> - Heading tags

\<br\> - Single line break

\<html\> - HTML document

\<strong\> - Defines important content

\<form\> - HTML form

\<audio\> - Defines audio content

HTML is the markup language. Most web designers use HTML with a combination of other markup and scripting languages to create web pages for a website. Typically, a web developer uses JavaScript, HTML, and CSS to build a website.

HTML websites are static. This means that the information does not change and it remains the same for every site visitor. The content of HTML websites is stored in static files. It has a static content, organization, and structure.

HTML websites require low or no maintenance. You do not need to regularly back up or install updates. You can just create a backup once and then, just forget about it. You do not need servers with installed PHP or MySQL. This means that the website can run on cheaper servers.

But HTML websites are very difficult to update. In fact, you'd need a formal training in programming to update an HTML website. You would need to hire a developer to make even the slightest changes like updating old content, adding new pages, or uploading images.

HTML websites have no additional features. If your business grows and you want to add an online store or a gallery, you would need to hire a developer to do this and that developer may recommend that you migrate your website to WordPress or some other variation of a PHP-driven website.

HTML websites operate on cheaper servers. But, since you need to hire a developer to do even the smallest tasks, the cost of maintaining an HTML website is usually higher than maintaining a PHP website.

PHP is a back-end scripting language. Today, the majority of websites runs on PHP because of the popularity of PHP content management systems (CMS) such as Joomla, Drupal, and WordPress. Websites that are built using the PHP are linked from an HTML file. A PHP code is enclosed in special start and end processing instructions such as <?php and ?>.

A PHP code looks like this:

```
<!DOCTYPE HTML>
<html>
        <head>
                <title>Example</title?>
        </head>
        <body>
                <?php
                        <echo "enter command";
                ?>
        </body>
</html>
```

PHP is executed on the server as opposed to client-side scripting language such as JavaScript. It is a back-end scripting language while HTML is a front-end markup language. This means that PHP uses HTML code as a structure.

PHP is very easy to use and learn especially if you are acquainted with the syntax or Perl or C. You can write a command using a few line codes. This gives you maximum control over your website. PHP is open source so it is free. You do not need to buy an expensive software to use it. It allows you to build a website at a minimal cost. It also has more functions than HTML.

It is cost efficient and reliable, too. It is also platform independent which means that it supports all major browsers and operating systems. It has faster processing speed than other scripting languages. So, it allows you to develop web apps like CRM or eCommerce. Using PHP is one of the most secure ways of developing websites and apps.

PHP is easy to read. This means that you do not have to be a coding genius to understand what the code is. It is clean and organized. It is also flexible so it's easier to add a new code without having to worry if it is in the correct place. It is easy to edit and it has better performace than most programming languages.

When you use PHP on your site, you don't have to think about programming so much. So, you can focus on the design of your site. And to top it all, it's free and easily available.

The main advantage of using a PHP-based website is that it has **dynamic content**. It is easy to update. You can simply log in to your WordPress site and add a new page without hiring a web developer. It has an intuitive user interface that makes it easy to update and create pages.

PHP-based websites such as WordPress have professional

ready-to-use templates that are developed by professionals all over the world. These sites are powerful. You can create contact forms, add a reservation system, and add a photo gallery by installing plugins. You can make whatever changes that you want.

HTML	PHP
Acronym of Hypertext Markup Language	Acronym of Hypertext Preprocessor
It is a markup language that cannot perform computations.	It is a general purpose programming language.
Front-end technology	Back-end technology
Used to create static sites	Used to create dynamic websites
HMTL-based websites are hard to modify.	PHP-based websites are easy to modify.
It is client-based.	It is server-based.
You need to hire a web developer to maintain your site and make changes.	You can make website changes yourself.
Too complicated.	Easier to learn and execute.

If you do not have all the technical training, it's best to use PHP-based websites. These websites are easy to use and navigate. You also do not need a skilled web designer to build your PHP site. You can simply use an open-source PHP software like WordPress to build and design your dream website.

Chapter Three

WordPress.com Versus WordPress On Your Own Hosted Domain Account

WordPress is an open-source publishing platform that makes it easier to publish content online. It powers millions of websites. There are two types of WordPress – WordPress.org and WordPress.com. The major difference between the two WordPress platforms is who's hosting your website.

When WordPress was initially launched, it was an open-source content management system. But, years after it was launched, Matt Mullenweg (the co-founder of WordPress) noticed that a lot of users are clamoring for a built-in WordPress hosting service. So, to meet this demand, he created WordPress.com – a managed and shared hosting services.

WordPress.com is a fully hosted website. It allows you to build your site free of charge if you choose the basic plan which goes with the ".wordpress.com" extension. You can also avail of the WordPress business hosting plan which comes with premium hosting, custom domain, and backups. This platform gives you access to hundreds of themes. It even allows you to install your custom theme.

If you are using a WordPress-hosted website, you can integrate your site with social networking sites such as Tumblr, Twitter, and Facebook. This site also comes with popular features such as comments, stats, polls, and sharing. If you use the basic site, there's no need to install plugins. To use a WordPress-hosted website, you have to register an account with WordPress.com.

When you use a WordPress-hosted website, you technically do not own the website. This means that WordPress can turn off your website if it goes against their terms of service.

WordPress.org is also known as the "real WordPress". It is a website platform that you can use on your own self-hosted website. It is open-source and it is free for anyone to use – you just need a web hosting account and domain name. This is the reason why WordPress.org is also known as a self-hosted WordPress. This allows you to get your hands dirty. You just need to purchase a domain name from a third party vendor like GoDaddy.com, sign up for a hosting account and install Wordpress within the account control panel.

The WordPress CMS is free and it is really easy to use. You own your website and its data. You do not have to worry about your site being turned off. You can customize your web design as needed. You can add paid, free, and custom WordPress plugin to your website.

The biggest advantage of running a self-hosted WordPress site is that you can actually use your site to earn money. You can run your own ads without sharing your revenues with someone else.

You can also use a self-hosted WordPress to build an online store. You can use it to sell physical or digital products. You can accept PayPal and credit card payments. You can also ship the goods directly from your website. You can also use this website to create membership sites. You can sell memberships for courses and content. You can also use it to build an online community.

WordPress.Com	WordPress.Org
WordPress.com is a hosting service.	WordPress is a content management system.
WordPress is free. But, you should adhere to the terms and conditions. WordPress can turn off your website anytime if they feel that your website is not following their guidelines.	WordPress.org is a software that you can download and install on your web server.
It comes with a free domain name called ".wordpress.com". You can also get a custom domain for a specific charge.	You would have to purchase the domain name from a third party provider.
WordPress.com comes with built-in features, but you cannot install plug-ins.	You can install plugins.
It comes with polished themes.	It comes with polished themes.

It comes with personal support. When you create a WordPress account, you also have access to WordPress forums. If you sign up for the premium plan, you'll get live chat and email support.	You need to visit the WordPress.org forums to ask for assistance.
You must register to build your WordPress.com account.	No registration needed.

So, which one should you choose? Should you go for WordPress-hosted website (WordPress.com) or a self-hosted WordPress website? Well, it depends. If you're into blogging, it's a good idea to get a WordPress-hosted website. But, if you plan to use your website for business, Defintely choose the self-hosted route.

Chapter Four

Domain Registration

In this section of the book, you'll learn all about domain registration. You'll know what a domain name is. You'll also learn the different domain name types and how to choose the right one for your website. This chapter also contains a step by step guide on how to purchase a domain name from one of the most popular domain registrars – GoDaddy.com.

Domain Name Explained

Each website has an address called domain name. Your website's domain name serves as the site identification. It identifies your internet resource – computer, service, or network. It is easier to memorize than the numbered addresses used in the internet protocols (IPs).

Domain names were created to make IP addresses more human friendly. The IP address is the unique set of numbers that are assigned to every computer on the internet. It is basically like a street address. They identify where a computer is located. A regular IP address looks like this – 191.179.3.95. It's not easy to memorize, right? While computers can easily identify IP addresses, we humans can use domain names.

The Domain Name System or DNS creates domain names that people easily understand like www.facebook.com or www.twitter.com. The DNS then translates that name to numbers so computers can understand them. So, instead of memorizing 66.220.144.0, you can simply type www.facebook.com. Easy, right?

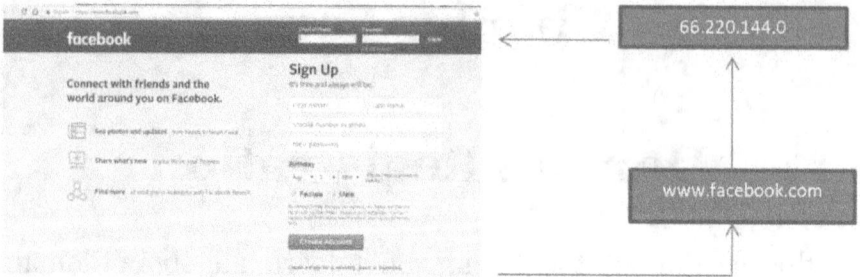

When people types your domain name in a web browser, the browser (such as chrome or internet explorer) uses your domain name to find your website IP address. Then, it passes back the website associated with that IP address.

Your domain name serves like the contacts that you store in your cellphone. So, when you tap the contact on your mobile phone, your phone automatically dials the number associated with that phone. You do not need to know where the person you're calling is located to enter their specific phone number. All you need to do is just tap the contact name and the phone does the rest.

The primary domain is simply the domain that you use to buy your server – like businessname.com. It is the name that you would register for your business or your website. A domain name is usually referred to as a primary domain or the top level domain. A primary or top level domain is a name that you choose to represent your business. It will be yours for a specific time (one year, five years, or ten years). Nobody else can touch it for that specific time.

You have the freedom to point this domain name to whatever site you want. You can use this name to represent you or your business. So, you have to pick a domain name that's short, stand-out, and easy to remember. It's also a good idea to pick a domain name with .COM as that's what people would generally associate with a business.

Once you have a primary domain, it's also a good idea to get a number of other domains as well to get more online traffic to your site. Adding secondary domain names also protects you from people who try to register your business name with other extensions to try to steal away your business. You can acquire a number of other domains. You can use .ORG to post internal company updates. You can use the .BIZ to showcase the business side of your company.

The first step in setting up and installing your self-hosted WordPress website is to make a decision about your domain name (which is also known as the unique resource locator or URL). Then, you have to purchase that domain name through a domain registrar. When you "buy" a domain, you really don't own it. You just earned the right to use it for a specific amount of time (one year or up to ten years).

Most domain registrars give you the choice to avail of a service called "autorenew". This automatically renews your domain once it expires and then charges the fee to your credit card.

Domain Syntax and Extensions

A URL typically has three parts:

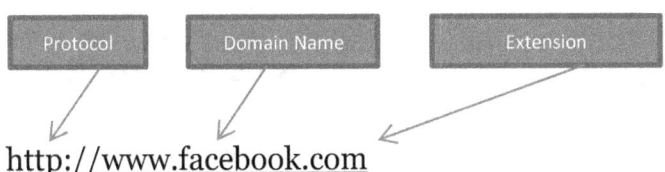

The protocol is how your browser should communicate with a server when opening your website. The most common protocol is HTTP or hypertext transfer protocol. Another common protocol is HTTPS, which means hypertext transfer protocol secure. The HTTPS protocol is usually used by e-commerce websites. There are also a number of less common protocols such as imap (internet message access protocol), pop (post office protocol), and ftp (file transfer protocol).

Domain Types

As discussed earlier, the domain name is the unique human friendly identification of your IP address. It has a domain extension that represents the purpose of your website or the location of your business.

Here's a list of the domain types:

1. **Generic Top Level Domains** – These domains are at the highest level of the domain name system structure. .COM is the most popular domain name extension. You should choose this extension if you want your website to look legit. More than fifty percent of websites use a .com extension.
2. **Generic Restricted Top Level Domains** – These domains are a bit similar to the generic top level domains, but the use is a bit restricted. For example, .BIZ is restricted to business and .PRO is reserved for accredited professional.
3. **Sponsored Top Level Domains** – These domains are sponsored and proposed by organizations and private agencies. It has strict rules on who could use these extensions. For example, .AERO is reserved for the members in the air transport industry.
4. **Country Code Top Level Domain or ccTLD** – Country code top level domain extensions are usually made of two characters such as .UK or .AU.
5. **Reserved Top Level Domains** – Top level domains such as .INVALID or .TEST are reserved by IANA or

Internet Assigned Numbers Authority.

6. **Second Level Domain** - This website type is below the top level domains. It usually contains two extensions. For example, universities may use the .AC.UK website extension, such as the University of Oxford website www.ox.ac.uk. Companies may use the .CO.UK extension, such as www.amazon.co.uk.

7. Third Level Domain – These domains are directly below the second level domain.

Examples of Country Code Domains

Zimbabwe	yourdomain.zw
Egypt	yourdomain.eg
South Africa	yourdomain.za
Belize	yourdomain.bz
Slovakia	yourdomain.sk
Switzerland	yourdomain.ch
Cook Islands	Yourdomain.ck
Zambia	yourdomain.zm
Samoa	yourdomain.ws
Vanuatu	yourdomain.vu
Andorra	yourdomain.ad
China	yourdomain.ca
Guam	yourdomain.gu

Armenia	yourdomain.am
Greece	yourdomain.gr
US Virgin Islands	yourdomain.vi
Uruguay	yourdomain.uy
Italy	yourdomain.it
British Virgin Islands	yourdomain.vg
Venezuela	yourdomain.ve
Germany	yourdomain.de
Hong Kong	yourdomain.hk
Spain	Yourdomain.es
Norway	yourdomain.no
Puerto Rico	yourdomain.pr
Cayman Islands	yourdomain.ky
Iceland	yourdomain.is
Iraq	yourdomain.iq
Philippines	yourdomain.ph
Kiribati	yourdomain.ki

Examples of Location-Based Second Level Domains

As mentioned earlier, second level domains have two extensions. The first extension usually indicates the website's function. The second extension contains the location of the website, e.g. www.greepeace.org.au. But, in some cases, the first extension represents the state where the organization is operating. The second extension indicates the country where the organization is located e.g. qld.au (for websites located in Queensland, Australia).

.asn.au	For associations, clubs, and political parties in Australia
.com.au	For business in Australia
.org.au	For the non profit organizations in Australia
.edu.au	For educational institutions in Australia
.act.au	For businesses and organizations located in Australian Capital Territory
qld.au	For businesses located in Queensland, Australia
.veterinaire.fr	For vets in France
.parliament.nz	For offices, parliamentary agencies, and political parties in New Zealand
.law.za	For lawyers and law firms in South Africa
.gov.ua	For government agencies in Ukraine

Tips on Choosing A Domain Name

Here's a list of tips that you can use in choosing a domain name:

1. *Make sure that it's easy to type.*

Choosing the right domain name is critical to the success of your business. So, make sure that your domain name is easy to remember and easy to type. Keep your domain name short and straight to the point.

2. *Insert keywords into your domain name.*

Keywords are the words or phrases that people use to find things on the internet. If you want your potential clients to easily find you, insert keywords in your domain name. For example, if your company name is Alva and you're selling shoes, it's a good idea to include "shoes" in your domain name. So, instead of "www.alva.com", you may want to go for "www.alvashoes.com". This way, it's easier for your potential customers to find you.

3. *Target your local area.*

If you run a local business, it's a good idea to include your city or state in your domain name. For example, if you run a plumbing company in Utah, you can choose www.utahplumbing.com as a domain name.

4. *Do not use hyphens and numbers.*

Hyphens and numbers are hard to type. So, as much as possible, avoid using them.

5. *Use the right domain name extension.*

Domain name extensions are suffixes found at the end of a website address such as .net or .com. These extensions have specific functions, so choose the one that works well for your company or organization.

The .com extension is the most popular one. But, it's kind of hard to get a memorable .com domain name because the best .com site names are already taken. So, you may want to consider the following alternative domain name extensions:

✓ .biz – You can use this if you're building an e-commerce site.

✓ .org – If you run a non-profit organization, you should consider this website extension.
✓ .net – This is for technical sites.
✓ .info – This extension is for informational sites.
✓ .co – This website extension is best for companies, communities, and even e-commerce sites.

6. *Use a domain name generator.*

If you really have a hard time coming up with a domain name, you can try domain name generators such as DomainHole, Lean Domain Search, or Wordoid.

If you are starting a personal website or a blog, it's a good idea to use your name. This will help you build your personal brand and make you more popular, if you are ok with putting your personal name out there like that.

How To Buy A Domain Name

There are a number of domain registrars that sell domain names such as GoDaddy, Sedo, Flippa, NameCheap, iPage, FatCow, Hover, Gandi, Dreamhost, and Name.com.

But, because GoDaddy is the most popular domain registrar today, let's discuss the step by step process of purchasing a domain using GoDaddy.com.

1. Log in to GoDaddy.com.

2. Now, type your desired domain name in the "find your perfect domain" space.

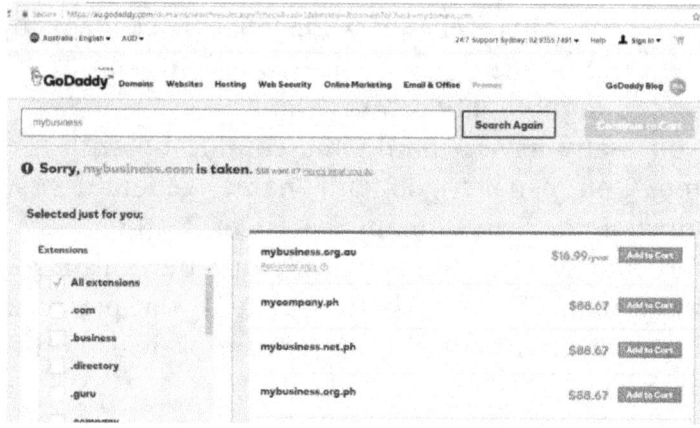

3. If your desired domain is already taken, you'll find suggested domain names on the left side of your screen.

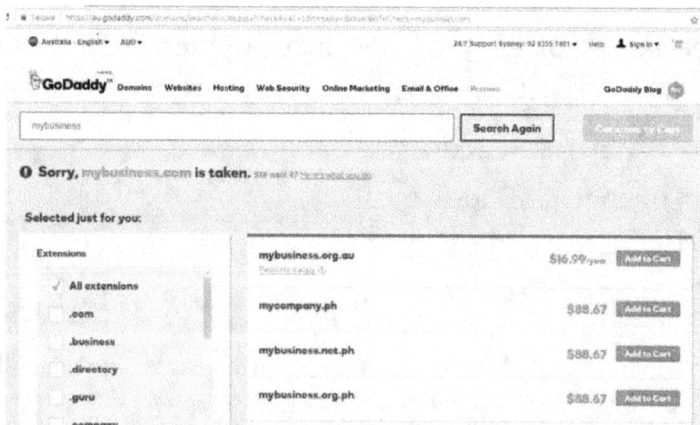

4. You'll see the price beside each domain name. Choose the one that fits best for your business and your budget.

5. Once you've chosen the right domain name, click on "add to cart". Then, click on the orange "continue to cart" button.

6. You'll see the web page below. If you want extra security, click on the Privacy Protection radio button. But, if you don't want any of that, just click on the radio button beside "No Thanks".

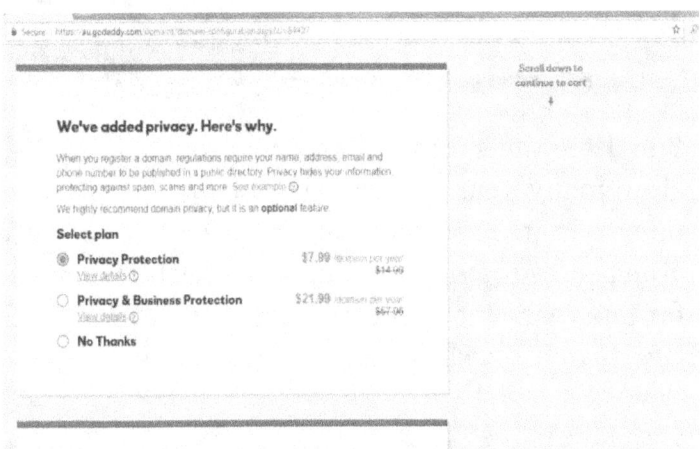

7. If you want to create an email that matches your domain, then scroll down and choose the email plan that's best for you. If not, choose "No Thanks".

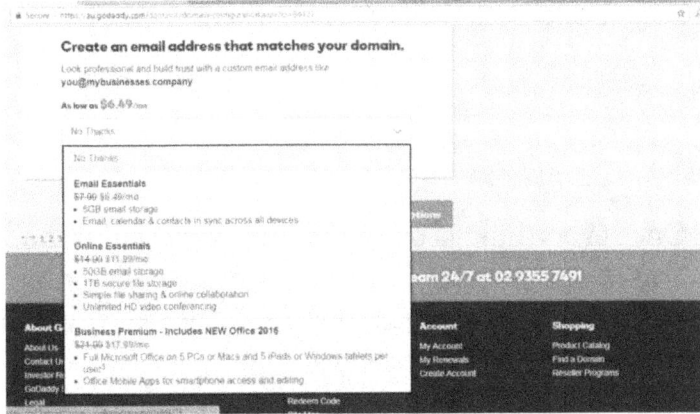

8. When you're done, click on "continue with these options".

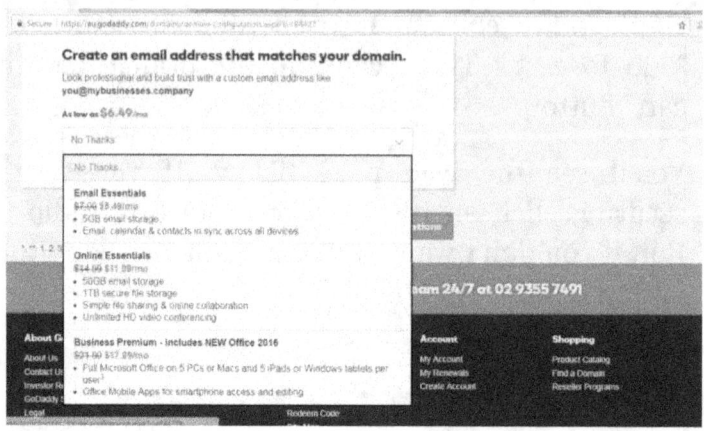

9. You'll see the summary of your order. Check the terms. How many years do you intend to own your domain name? Is it one year? Or two years? If you're not too attached to the domain name, you can choose to rent it for one year. But, if you feel like you'd need it in the long run, then it's best to rent it for two years or more.

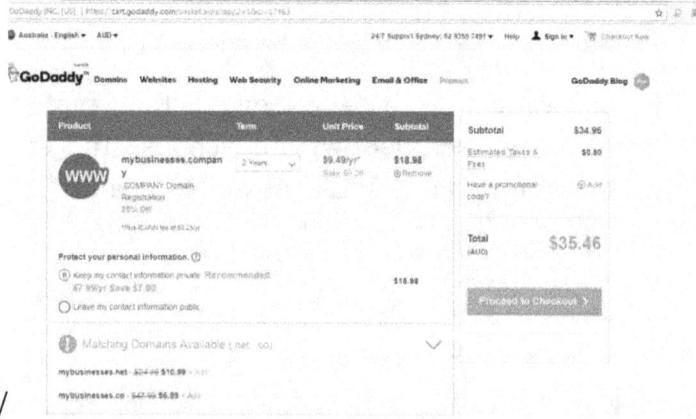

10. Once everything is okay, click on "proceed to checkout".
11. You'll need to sign in to proceed with the order. If you do not have an existing GoDaddy account, you have to click on "create an account".

12. Now, after you created an account, you'll need to pay for your order. You can pay using a credit card, a debit card, or PayPal.

13. Now, once you've entered your payment info, you're good to go. You now own your domain name for a specific amount of time.

Now, that you've successfully acquired a domain name, it's time to choose a web hosting provider.

<u>Chapter Five</u>

Select A Web Hosting Provider and Set-Up Your Hosting Account

To make your website visible on the internet, your data and files must be stored in a computer that's connected to the internet. These computers are called web servers. Website hosts are companies and organizations that house several web servers in one location. This is often called a data center.

Hosts provide the security, tools, support, and bandwidth that connect your website to the internet. It is like a mall that contains several stores. If you want to open a shop at a mall, you need to lease a space. Just like a mall, hosting companies allow you to lease a space in their web servers where you can store your website files and make them available for visitors.

Web hosts offer a number of hosting solutions. You can choose the one that fits your server space need and the amount of "bandwidth" that you would need each month. Bandwidth is simply the amount of data being transferred at a given amount of time.

If your website does not need a lot of space, then you can rent a small server space. But, beyond server space and bandwidth, there are other things that you should consider in selecting a hosting solution. You need to consider your budget and the ease of use. You also need to consider the level of flexibility and customization. You may also want to consider the privacy and security features in choosing the right hosting solution for your website.

Types of Web Hosting Solutions

There are four main types of hosting solutions:

1. Shared Hosting – If you choose a shared hosting solution, your account is one of the many accounts on a server that's maintained by a hosting company. A shared server is like an apartment building with several tenants. This hosting solution is cheaper. But, an influx of traffic to one website on the server will affect the bandwidth of the other websites. So, this is a good choice for low-traffic websites.

   If you have a limited budget, shared hosting may be the best option. This solution is perfect for a website that does not have more than two thousand visitors daily.

2. Virtual Private Servers or VPS – A VPS, as the name suggests, is a virtual server that's private. Unlike shared hosting, a VPS hosting has a guaranteed allotment of system and resources that only you have access to, but everyone is still on the same physical machine/host.

3. Dedicated Hosting – Dedicated server hosting is best for websites that generates a lot of traffic daily like Facebook or Twitter. It is known as the "Rolls Royce" of web hosting. If shared hosting is like renting an apartment and VPS is like renting a townhouse, dedicated hosting is like renting an entire house.

   It is a step above VPS hosting. It is also the most expensive type of hosting. So, unless your website is drawing at least one hundred thousand visitors per day, it's not practical to choose dedicated hosting.

4. Cloud Hosting – Cloud hosting is a hosting service where the files are stored in the cloud. If you choose cloud hosting, your files are backed up in multiple locations. What's amazing about cloud hosting is that

you only pay for what you use. But, it is prone to service outages. So, you would expect some downtime every now and then. Also, you have limited control over your services, data, and applications.

Shared hosting is cheap. It is perfect for small businesses. If you want to establish a website for less that $25, it's best to go for shared hosting. But, if you're looking to attract a lot of visitors in the future, it's a good idea to choose VPS hosting. It is less expensive than the dedicated server, but it gives you all the bandwidth that you need.

Best Hosting Providers

Web hosting is now becoming a common commodity. It's no wonder that the number of hosting companies increases by the minute. But, here's a list of the most reliable web hosting providers:

1. HostGator

HostGator offers shared hosting plans for as low as $2.99 per month. Plus, they have an uptime of around 99.98%. They also have a friendly and proactive technicians that provide support. They have a user friendly control panel and a free site builder. They also offer a 45 day money back guarantee.

2. BlueHost

Most BlueHost plans come with a free site builder and domain. They adhere to the highest hosting hardware. They also have an awesome customer support team.

3. Site Ground

This web hosting provider offers plans that include CDN, email, SSL, and daily backups. Their lowest plan has about 10 GB web space and it is suitable for websites with ten thousands visits per month.

4. InMotion Hosting (#1 Author's Pick)

InMotion Hosting is convenient because it comes with preinstalled WordPress. Their plans usually include unlimited bandwidth and a free SSL certificate. They have solid reputation and they have a team of friendly and competent customer service staff.

5. HostPapa

This company provides affordable, but reliable web hosting that uses green energy. They offer user-friendly tools that anyone can use. They also have an impressive 99.9% uptime. Then, they have a thirty day money back guarantee.

6. Dream Host

Dream Host has been around for almost two decades. Up until today, they are still one of the most reliable web hosting providers. They power over five hundred thousand WordPress blogs. They do not collect a set-up fee and they offer a free domain, too.

7. GreenGeeks

They have a hosting platform that's easy to install and manage. They provide a 24-hour support and they come with free domain name.

8. A2

A2 provides fast and reliable WordPress hosting. They also have a team of technical experts that can help with your needs.

9. Pagely

This is the largest WordPress hosting platform and it is now powered by Amazon cloud. They are used by big companies such as Twitter, Facebook, and Microsoft.

10. GoDaddy

Yes, GoDaddy offers hosting, too, that costs only $1 a month! Their yearly plan also comes with a free domain. It's awesome, isn't it?

11. Site5

This web hosting provider offers special plans for those who are new to WordPress. They offer superb support and service. Their servers are located in various cities around the world including London, Sydney, Singapore, and Amsterdam.

12. Ipage

This company was established in 1998 and they have been providing reliable and fast hosting services since then. They offer unlimited hosting that comes with a free domain.

Purchase Your Hosting and Set Up Your Hosting Account

There's a long list of reliable web hosting provider which includes Hostgator, A2 Hosting, SiteGround, Bluehost, Ehost, A Small Orange, Site5, and InMotion. For the purposes of discussion, let's discuss how you can purchase and set up an InMotion hosting account.

1. Go to the website of your web host provider. In this case, go to www.inmotionhosting.com.

2. Click on "get started" now.

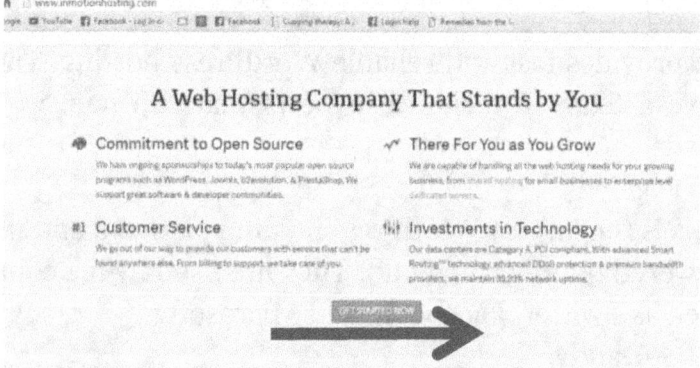

3. This will take you to the shared hosting options. Choose the option that works well for you and then click on "order now".

4. VPS is a better option, especially if you're planning to establish a high traffic website. Go to www.inmotionhosting.com/vps-hosting if you wish to

purchase VPS hosting. But, please take note that this is expensive. So, unless you're planning to create a website that attracts as much traffic as Buzzfeed, it would be a good idea to go for shared hosting. You can always upgrade your hosting plan later on.

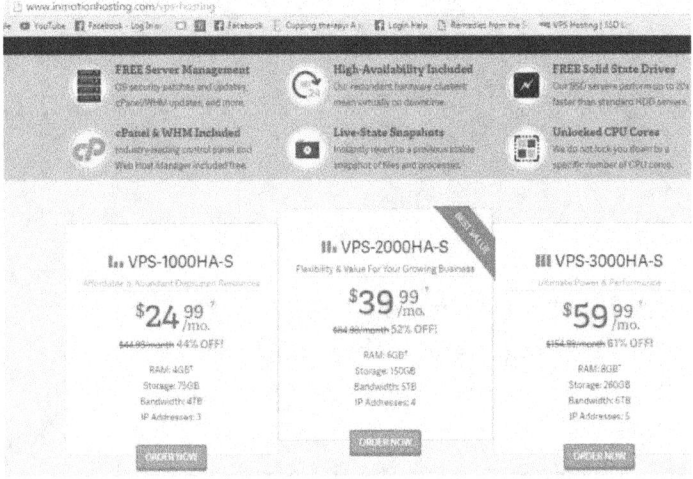

5. Select your preferred hosting term. You could either purchase 1 month, 6 months, or 1 year hosting.
6. Choose the data center you like (East Coast or West Coast).

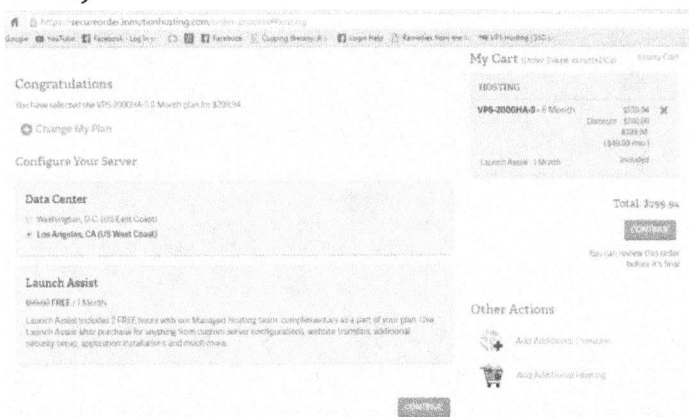

7. Click on "I already own this domain" and enter your domain.
8. Enter your email address and click on "continue".

9. Fill up your billing information.

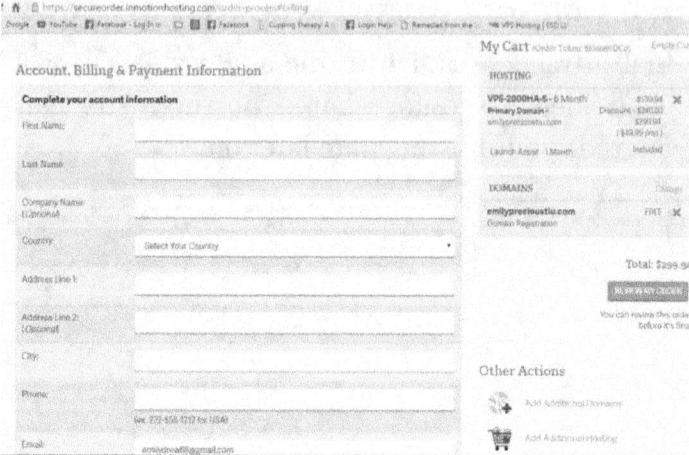

10. Click on "review my order".
11. If everything is good, then you're done.
12. Log in to your account management panel.
13. Go to www.inmotionhosting.com. Click on "log in" at the top right corner of your screen.
14. Since this is your first time to log in, click on "click here".

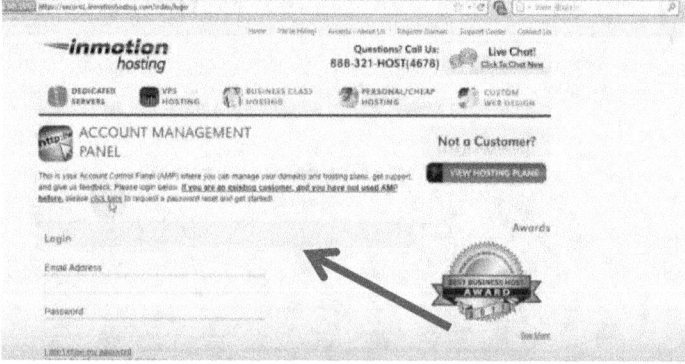

15. This will take you to the "forgot password" page. Enter your domain name and your email address, then click on submit. You'll receive a password reset link through email.
16. Check your email and click on the link. This will take you to this page.

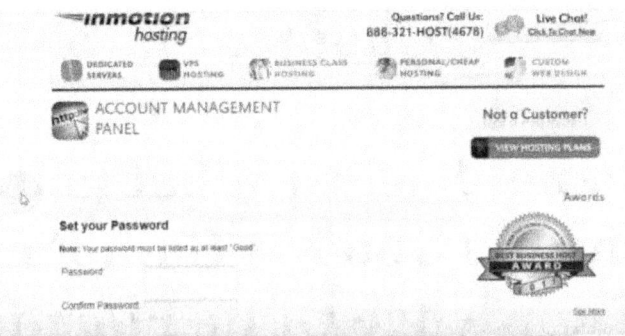

17. Enter your new password and click submit.

18. Click on the log in link. Then, type your email address and your password.

19. Now, you're logged in to your account management panel! This allows you to create a cPanel account and then easily manage your website.

The Account Management Panel or AMP is the gateway that gives you access to any tool that you need. This allows you to update your billing information, access your cPanel, install software, and renew your subscriptions. Remember that your AMP contains your credit card number and other billing information. Do not give this information to your web developer or someone you don't trust.

Chapter Six

cPanel Basics: What Is It and Why It's Good to Gain Further Knowledge Of Its Functions

cPanel is a linux-based online hosting control panel. It has a graphical interface and tools that are intended to streamline the web hosting process. It uses a three layer structure that allows the web developers and owners to control the different parts of their blog or website. cPanel is designed to function as a virtual private server or a dedicated server.

It is the industry-standard and it is used by most web hosting companies. It makes web hosting account management easier. It is easy to install and also easy to use. You don't need to be a coding genius to learn how to use cPanel.

It is a low-maintenance program and it only requires 20GB disk space. It has a top notch email management function. It also comes with anti-virus and anti-fraud protection.

So, what does cPanel do? Well, it helps create and manage e-mail address. It also allows you to create and manage files. It also helps you create and manage databases.

Benefits of cPanel

cPanel is amazing. It is free and it's used by Linux-based web hosting. Here's a list of the cPanel benefits that you can use to your advantages:

1. It is easy to install and use.

You do not need to be a computer genius to install and use this web hosting management system. It has an intuitive graphical interface that allows you to do tasks like looking for web directories, calculating disk space, making regular back-ups, and site maintenance in just a few clicks.

2. It saves money.

Because it is easy to use, you do not have to hire people to maintain your site. You can do it yourself. So, you'll definitely save a lot of money on labor costs.

3. It's compatible with all browsers.

You can run this program using any browser – Chrome, Safari, Mozilla Firefox, or Internet Explorer.

4. It's compatible with software add-ons.

What's amazing about this hosting management system is that it's compatible with third party software add-ons. It supports apps and add-ons such as calendars, guest books, bulletin boards, and blogs.

5. It's reliable.

cPanel is so reliable that it automatically restart the system once it detects a failed service. It also has a domain name system (DNS) clustering system. This improves the performance of your hosting system and minimizes downtime.

6. It's portable.

This is one of the most amazing features of the cPanel. It is moveable. This means that you can move your website from one hosting company to another without any problem.

How To Create A cPanel Account

Now we know how awesome cPanel is. But, how do you login to your "cPanel"? Well, it's kind of easy. You just have to follow these steps:

1. First, log in to your hosting account management panel. If you're using InMotion hosting, log in to secure.inmotionhosting.com/index/login.

2. Then, click on the cPanel icon.

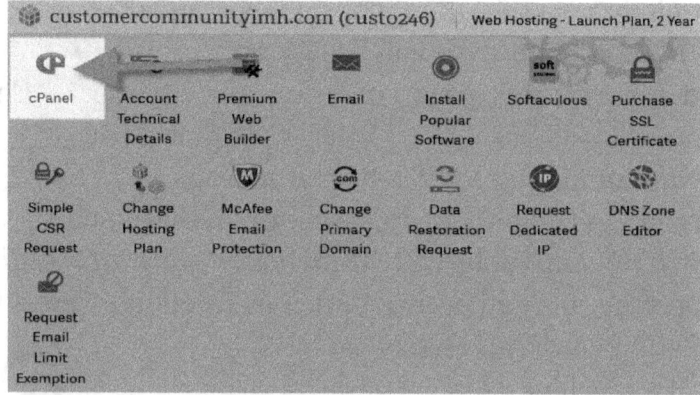

3. This will take you straight to your cPanel. You do not need to enter a username or password.

4. If it does ask you for a username and password. Just click on "back" and then click on the "account technical details" button.

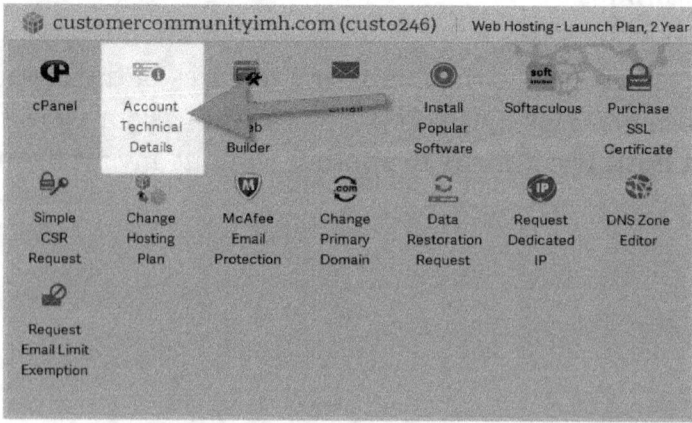

5. You'll see your username and password. Take note of that and then, click on the cPanel icon. Use your username and password to log in.

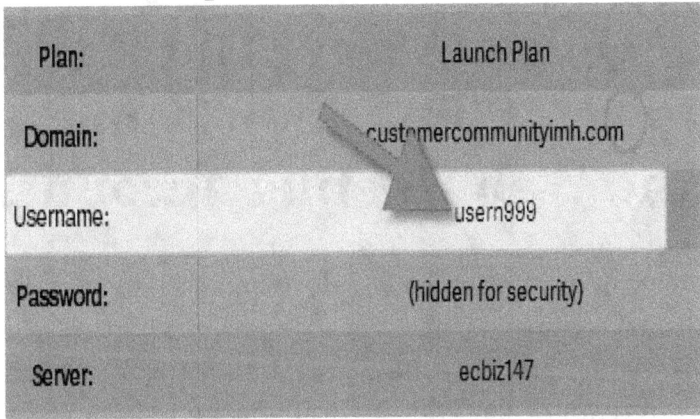

Plan:	Launch Plan
Domain:	customercommunityimh.com
Username:	usern999
Password:	(hidden for security)
Server:	ecbiz147

If you're working with a team of web developers and bloggers, it's best to log in to cpanel by typing **yourdomainname.com/cpanel**. Then, you'll see this page.

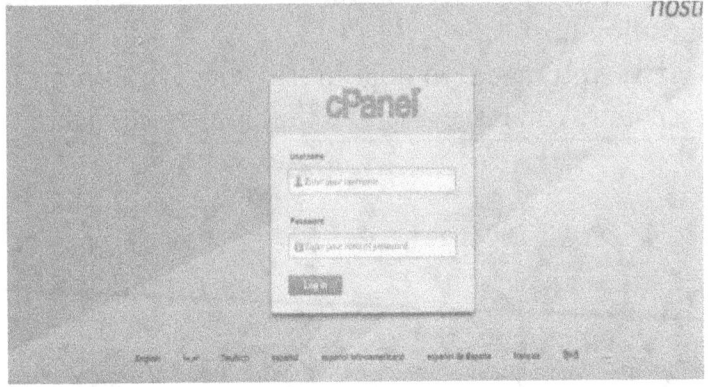

If you have not pointed your domain name to your web host server yet, type this in your web browser yourservername.yourdomainname.com/cpanel, example ezbiz143.example.com/cpanel. Then, enter your username and password.

Chapter Seven

Quick CPanel Tutorial (How to Point Your Domain to the Web Hosting Account)

Now that you have purchased a domain and you already have a web host, it's time to point your domain to your web hosting account. You need to follow two basic steps – change the nameservers and then add the domain name to your web host server. The good news is it just takes a few minutes to do this.

In the earlier sections of this book, we discussed how to purchase a GoDaddy domain name and use InMotion hosting. So, now, let's discuss how to point your GoDaddy domain to your InMotion hosting.

1. First, you need to log in to your InMotion hosting account. You'll see a screen that looks like this:

2. Go to your "cPanel".

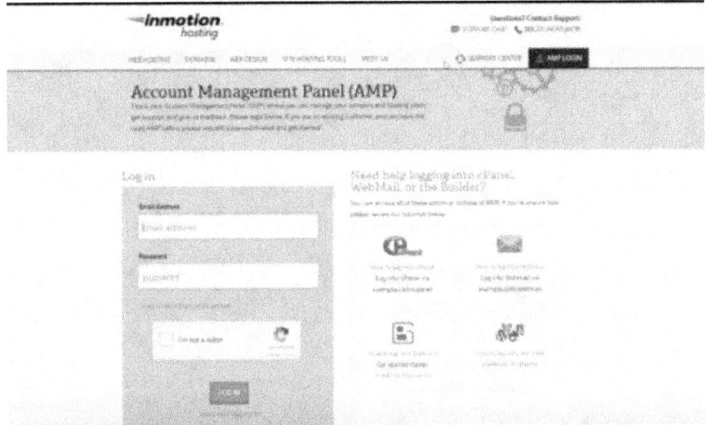

3. You'll see this:

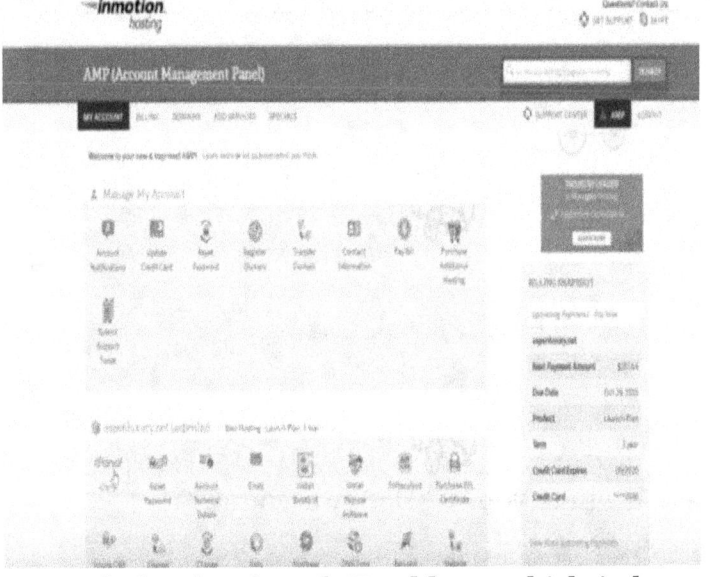

4. Look for the shared IP address which is located at the bottom left part of your screen.

5. Highlight and copy the IP address at the lower left side of your screen.

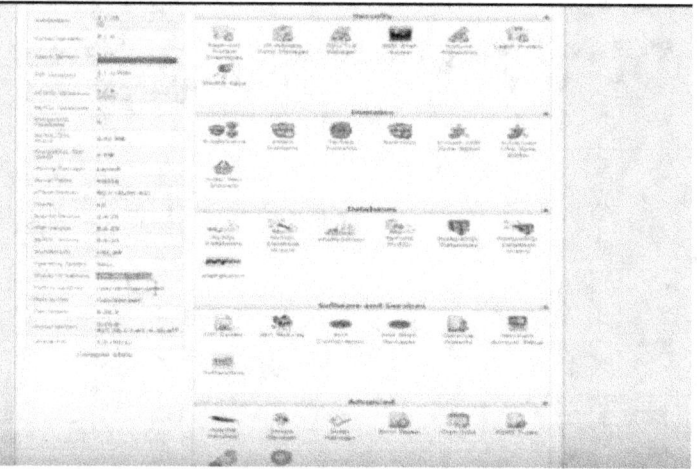

6. Then, log in to your GoDaddy account.

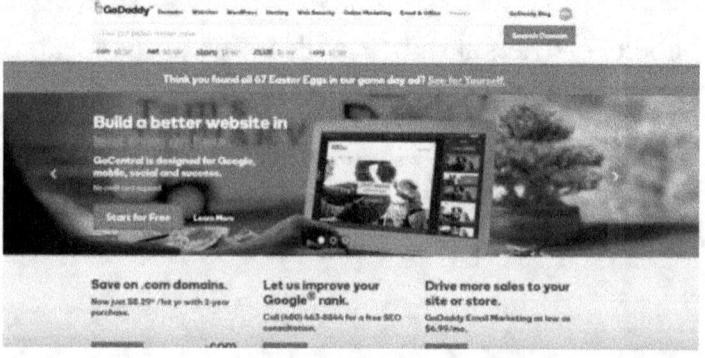

7. Click on the drop down menu beside your name.

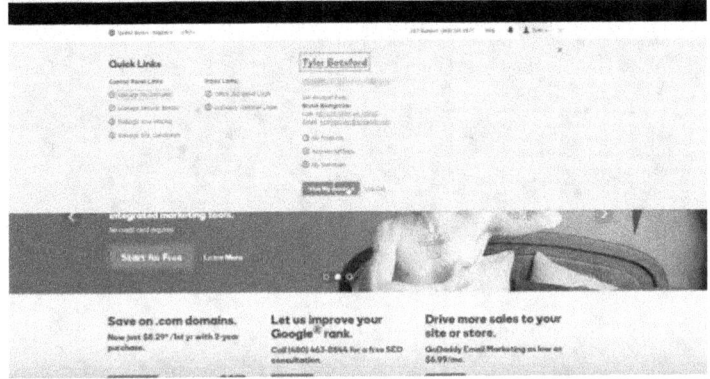

8. Click on the green "visit my account" button to pull up your domain names.

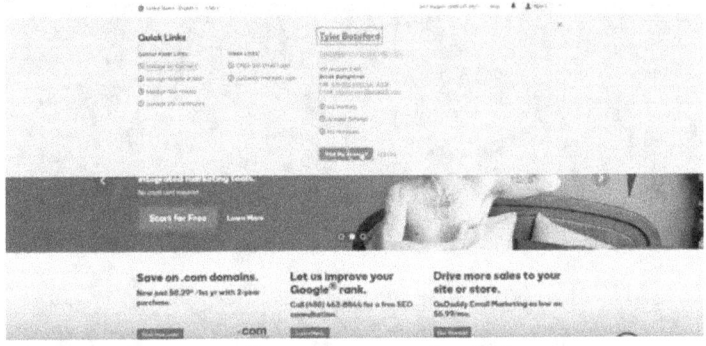

9. Click on "manage" to see your domain names.

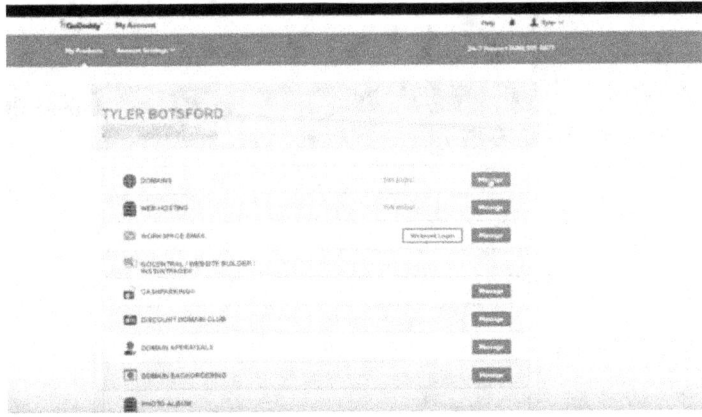

10. Type the domain name you want to direct on the search tab at the upper right side of your screen. Then, click on

"search".

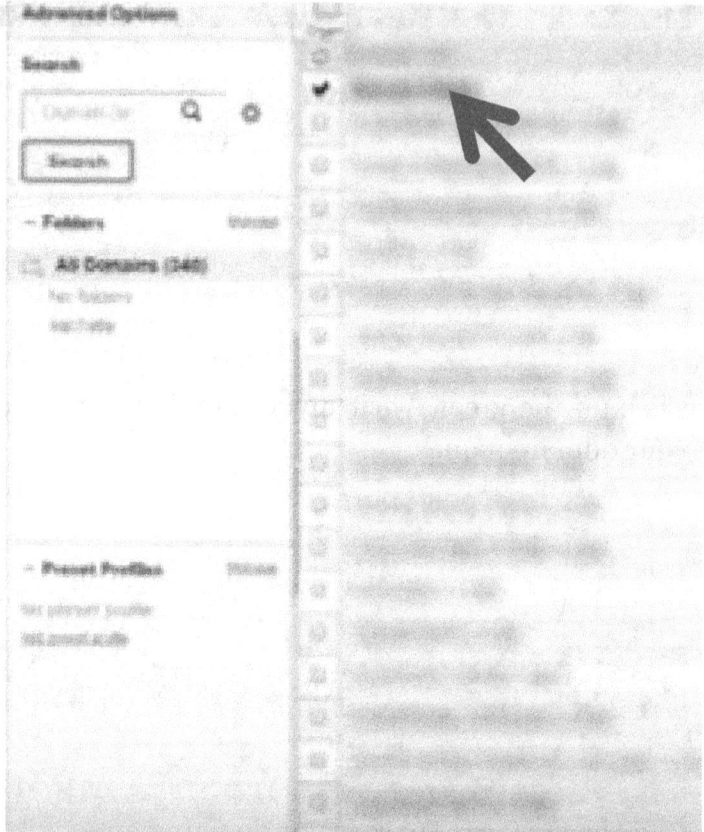

11. Click on the drop down next to the domain name.

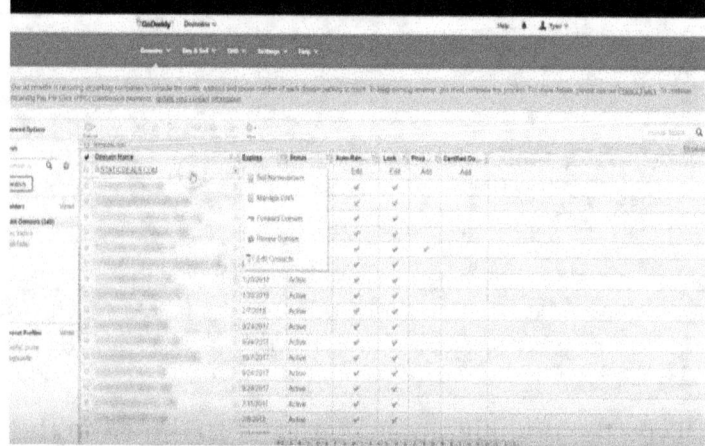

12. Click "manage DNS".

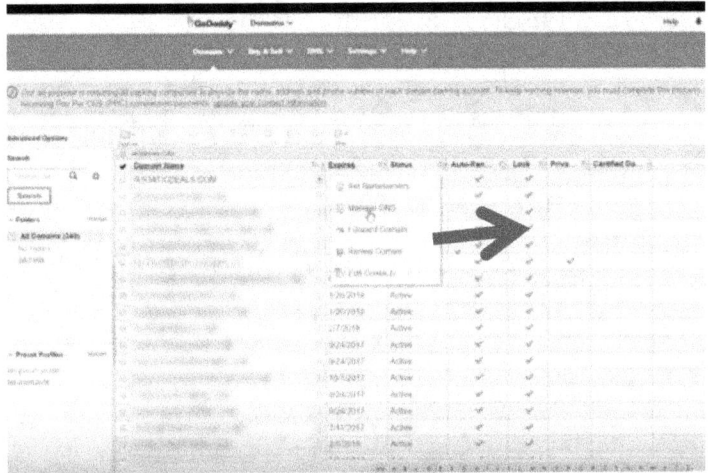

13. You'll see the DNS records of the chosen domain name.

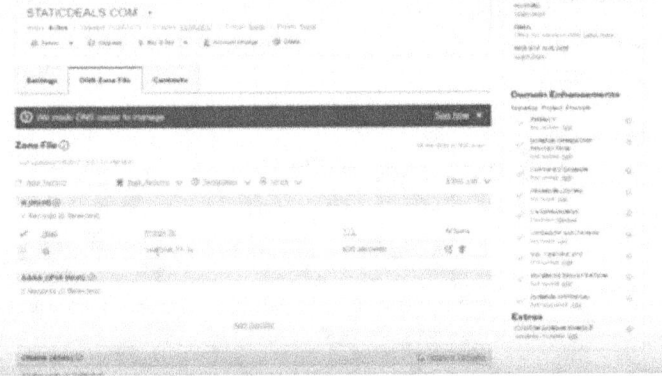

14. Look at the "host record" section and then click on "edit".

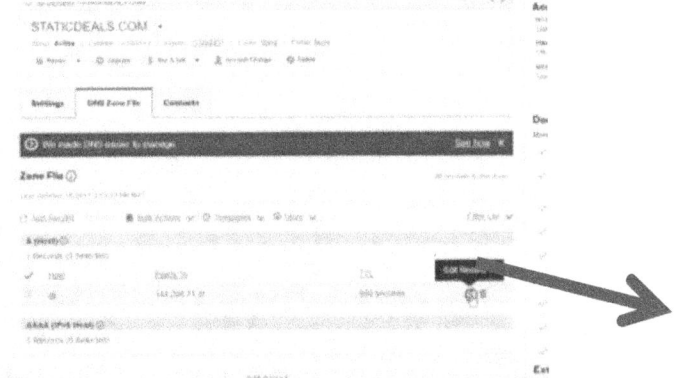

15. Under "host to", paste the IP address from your InMotion hosting account.

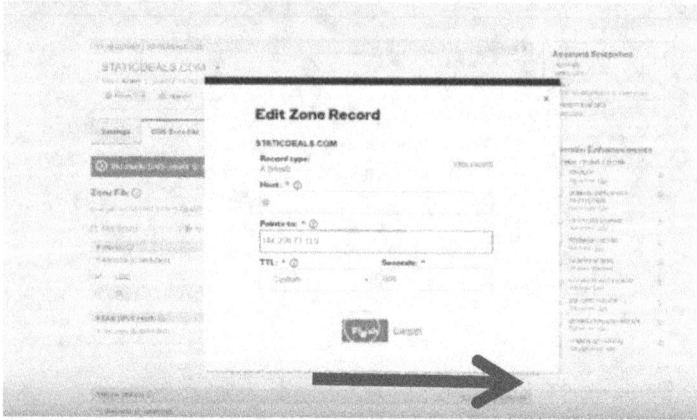

16. Click on "finish".
17. Then, click on "save changes".
18. Your domain name is now on your InMotion hosting account.
19. Go back to your cPanel.
20. Click on "addon domains" button.

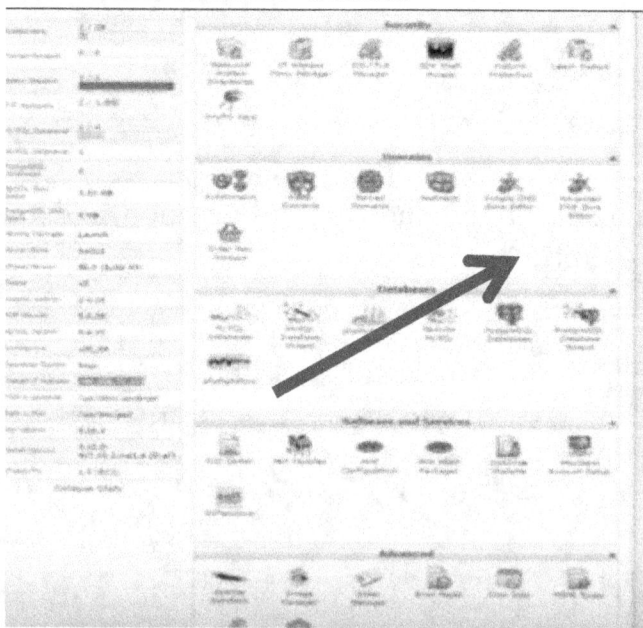

Source: greenmonkeymarketing.com

21. Click on the domain name you want to add.

Now that you have successfully added your domain name to your hosting account, it's time to install WordPress.

Chapter Eight

cPANEL: Making A Database In MySQL

cPanel allows you to create and manage a database. You can use this database to run a website and store files.

To create a database in MySQL, you need to follow these steps:

1. Go to your "cPanel".
2. Under databases, click on MySQL database.

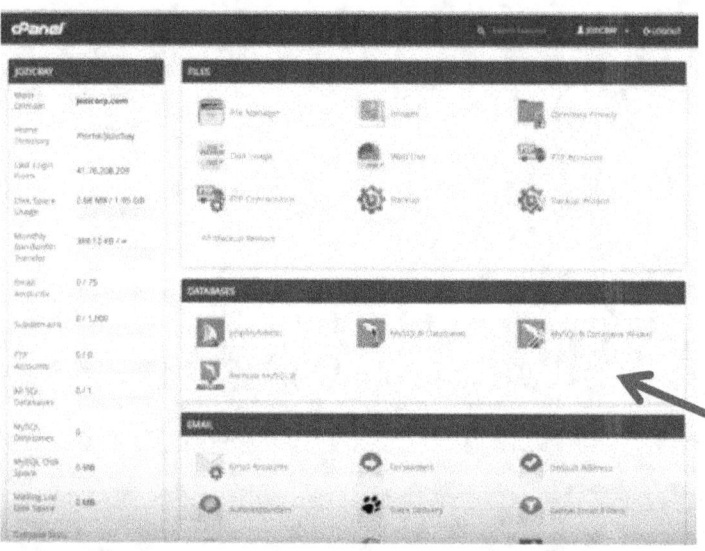

3. You'll see this page.

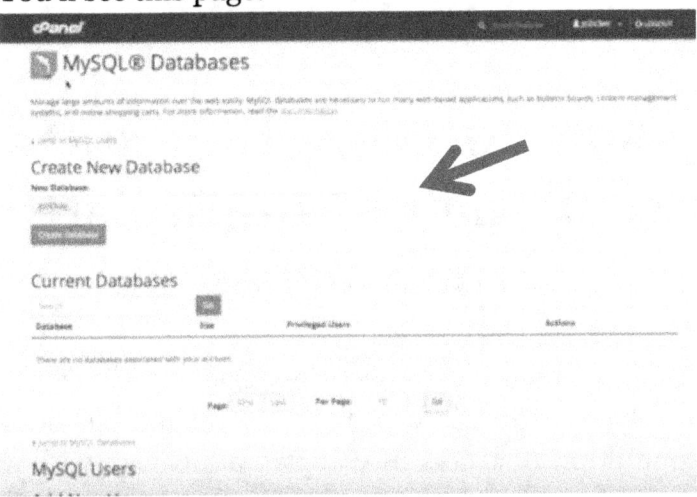

4. Enter the name of your database and then, click on "create database".

5. You'll see this page. Enter your desired username and password. Then, click on create user.

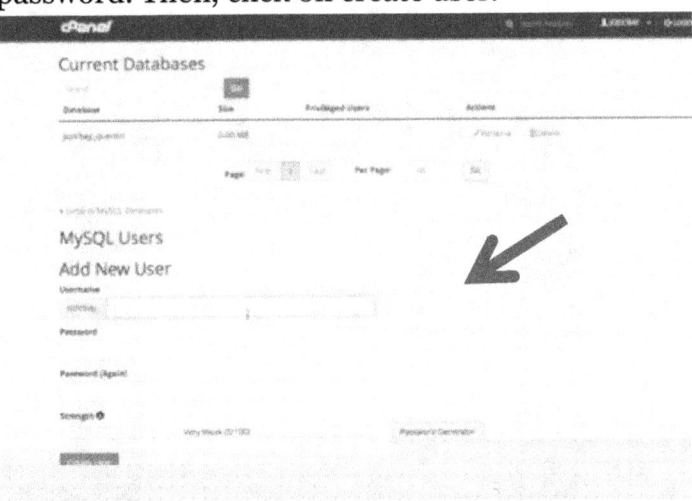

6. If you want to add more users in your database, you can click on "add users". You can always remove these users anytime you want.

You're done. It's that simple!

Chapter Nine

CPANEL: How to Add-On More Domains You Register To Your Account

You can operate multiple websites/domains in your cPanel account. This feature is especially useful for businesses that operate multiple websites. If you own a business with multiple brands, you need to add more domains to your hosting account by following these steps:

1. Go to your "cPanel". Enter your username and password.

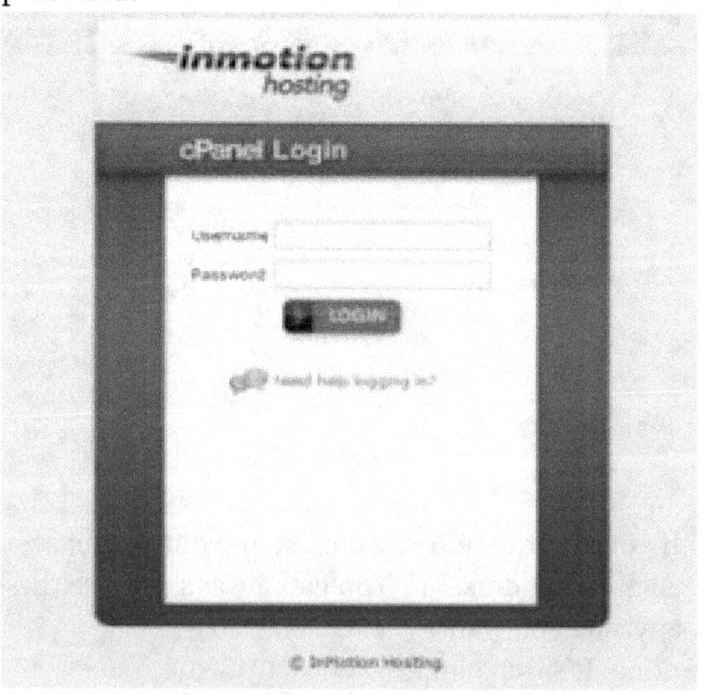

2. Go to the "domains" section.

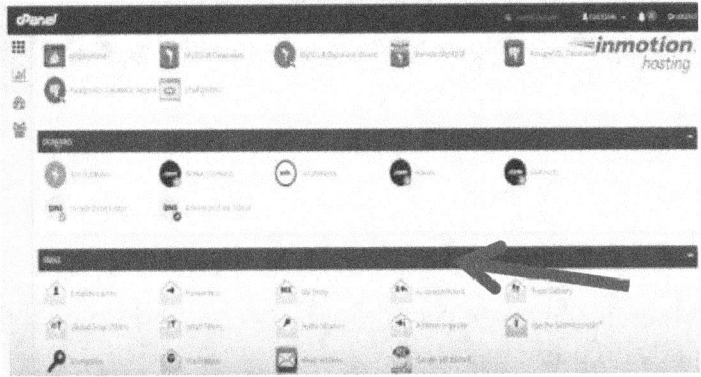

3. Click on the "addon domains" button.

4. Under create an addon domain, enter the domain name that you're going to add to your cPanel account.

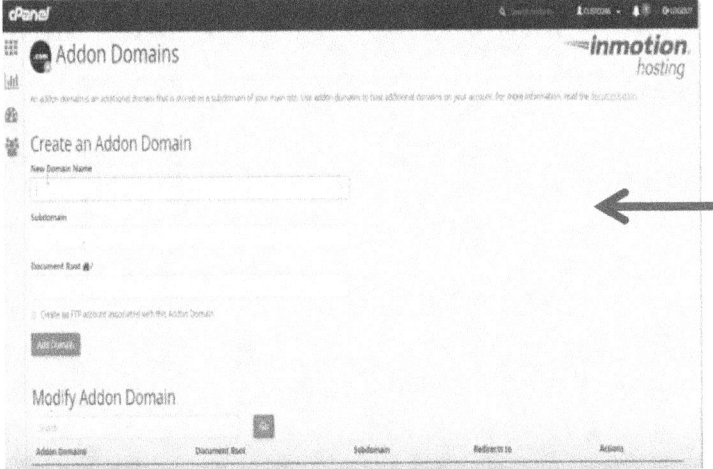

5. There's a default subdomain so you won't need to type a subdomain name.

6. You'll need to enter the "document root". This is the folder where you store the files of your domain, ex. public_html/domain.com.

7. Click on the button that says "create FTP account". This is helpful if you are working with a web developer who needs FTP access.

8. Click the "add domain" button.
9. You'll see this page.

10. If you click on back, you'll see your domain listed on addon domains.

You're done! You're ready to set-up your other website.

Chapter Ten

How To Install WordPress Using Softaculous

Earlier in this book, we've discussed how useful it is to install WordPress in your self-hosted website. In this chapter, you'll finally learn how to install WordPress on your website using a wonderful tool called softaculous.

Softaculous is an amazing tool that runs on your cPanel or other control programs such as Plesk and DirectAdmin. It allows you to install a number of customer support software, eCommerce software, and blogging platforms. It also allows you to install WordPress on your self-hosted website. You can do this by following these steps:

1. Go to your "cPanel".

2. After you log in, scroll down and go to the software services section.

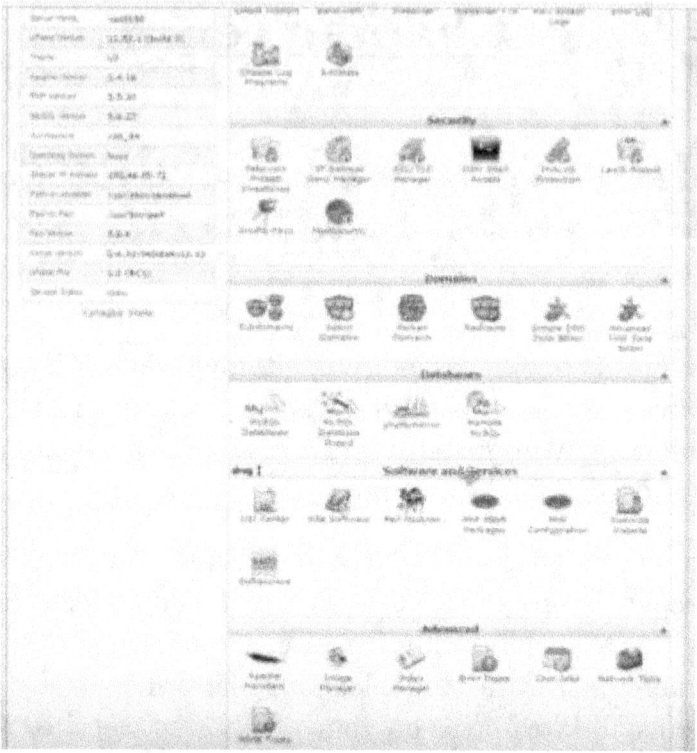

3. Click on the "softaculous" button.

4. You can see the top applications in Softaculous and click on the WordPress icon.

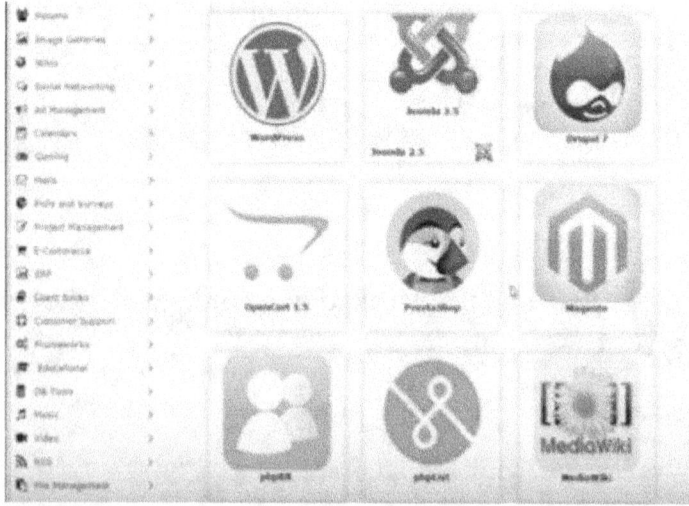

5. Then, click on the "install" button.

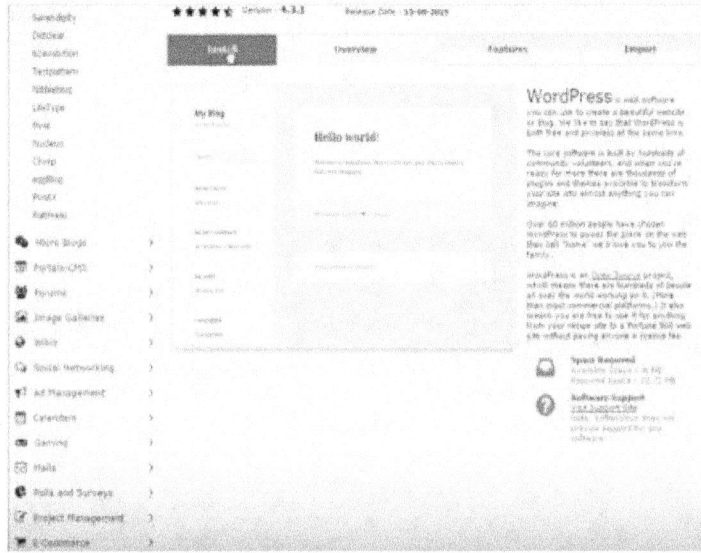

6. Under "choose protocol", you have the option to choose between the following options:

    *   http://
    *   http://www.
    *   https://
    *   https://www.

    You can go with whatever you like. The https option provides added security to your website. But, you would need to purchase an SSL certificate to use this protocol. We will discuss this later in the bonus section of this book.

7. Below the "choose protocol", you'll see "choose domain". If you have multiple domains in your hosting account, you'll need to choose the website where you want to install WordPress.

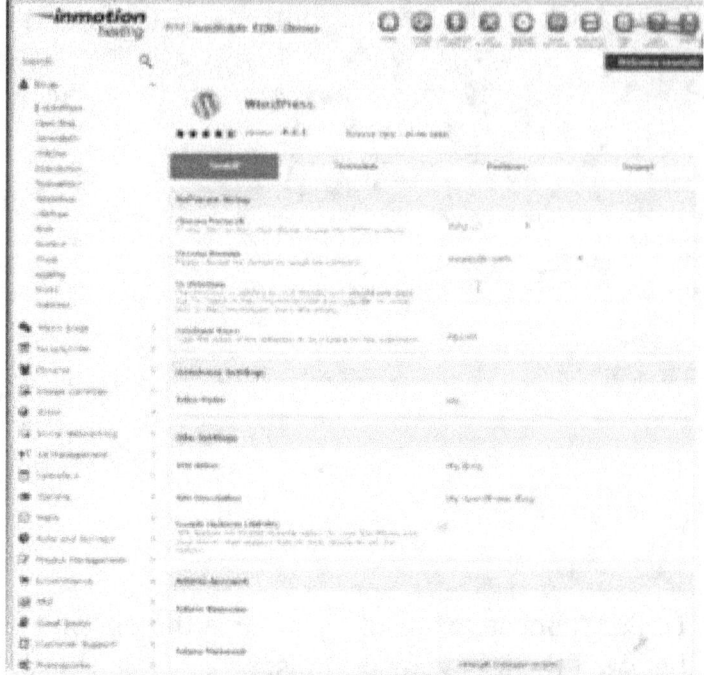

8. Leave the "in directory" section blank.
9. Enter your database name under the "database name" section. The name usually starts with wp_, ex. wp_01.
10. Under site settings, enter your website name.

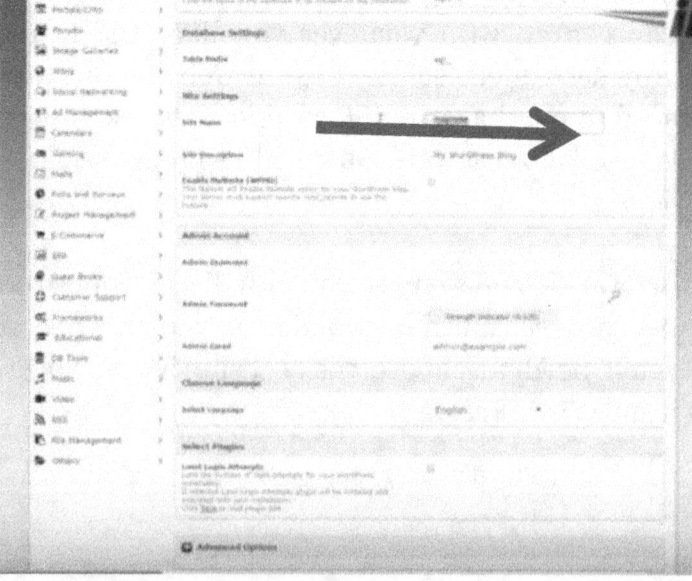

11. Enable multisite if you plan to operate multiple blogs in your website. We will discuss this feature later on in the bonus section of this book. If you decide to use the "multisite" feature, make sure to use plugins that are compatible with multisite.

12. Enter your desired admin username and password. This is what you'll use when you log in to your WordPress CMS and dashboard. Make sure to use a unique admin name and a strong password. We will discuss the password rules under the bonus section of this book.

13. Enter your admin email. You'll get an email every time someone comments on your blog or there's updates available.

14. Choose the language you want to use.

15. Under select plugins, click on the "limit login attempts". This feature can protect your website from hackers by limiting the login attempts. You can also install this plug in later, after you complete the installation process.

16. **Click on the "advanced option". You'll see a number of options there. Should you want WordPress to automatically upgrade your themes, click on "auto upgrade WordPress themes". If you want WP to automatically upgrade your plugins once a new WP version comes out click on "auto upgrade WordPress plugins". You can add these options later after installation.** We'll discuss this process later in the bonus section of this book.

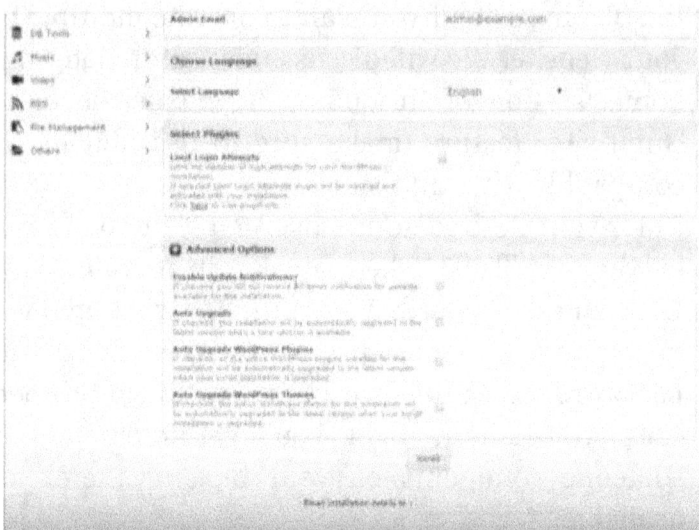

17. After you've chosen all of your preferred options, click on the "install" button located at the bottom part of your screen.

18. Below the install button, enter your email address so you'll get a notification once the installation is complete.

19. The installation takes a few minutes. Once it's complete, you'll see this page.

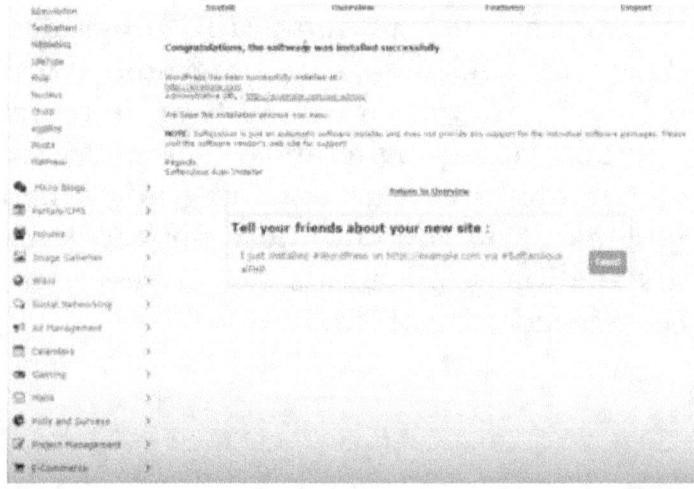

20. You'll see a link that points to your website. When you click it, you'll see this clean and blank installation of WordPress.

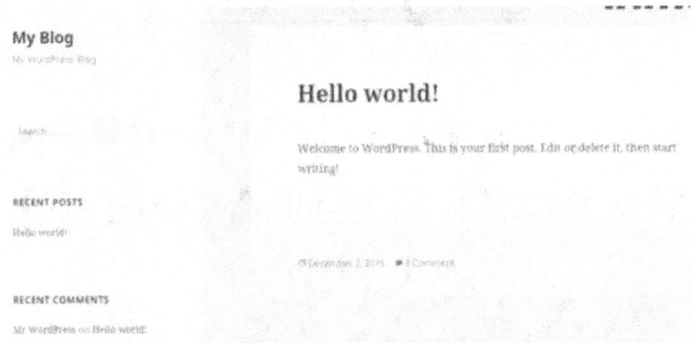

21. You'll also find your admin URL. This is where you log in to your posts and manage your blog, photos, and other content. When you click on that URL, you'll see this:

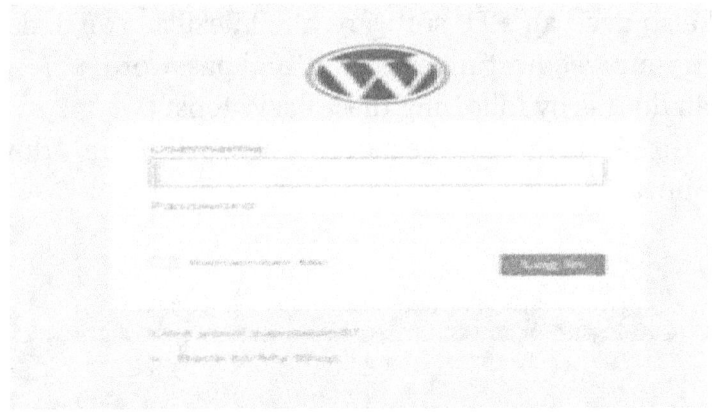

Log in using your admin name and password. Now, you can start creating your website content!

Chapter Eleven

How To Install WordPress Manually Using A Free FTP Utility

It's quite easy to install WordPress by using your cPanel. You can also install it using a free FTP utility like **Filezilla**. But, to do this, your web host must be able to support MySQL and PHP. You'll also need the ability to create MySQL databases. You'll also need an FTP software like Filezilla. You'll also need to have your web hosting username and password.

You can do this by following these easy steps:

1. Go to filezilla.project.org. Then, click on "download now".

2. Then, install it on your computer.
3. Now, you'll need to get a hold of the WordPress files. To do that, go to wordpress.org. Then, click on "Download WordPress".

4.

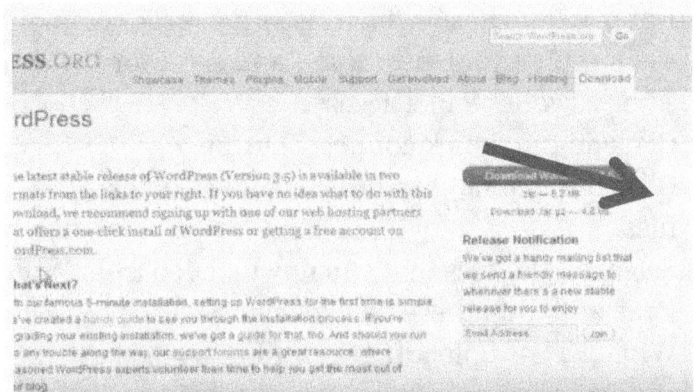

5. Download WordPress to your computer.
6. Go to your web hosting panel by typing yourdomainname.com/cpanel in your web browser. Scroll down and make sure that you can see the "MySQL Databases".

7. Unzip your WordPress files.

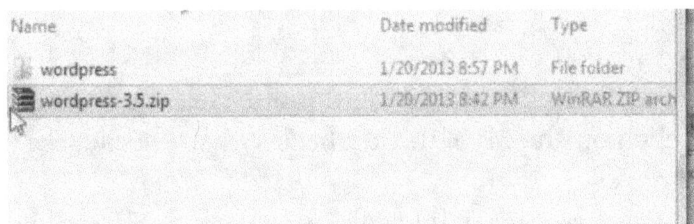

8. Now, you're going to see this.

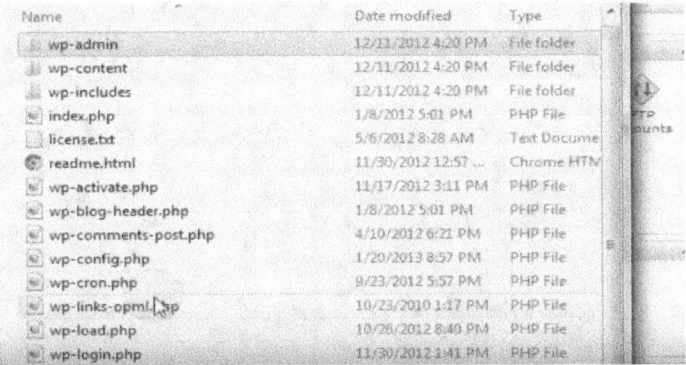

9. Select all the files. Then, go to FTP filezilla.

10. Enter your host which is <u>ftp.yourdomainname.com</u>. Then, enter your username and password which is the same as your cPanel access.

11. Click on the "quick connect" button.

12. Click on public_html. This folder holds your website files.

13. Select all the files that you downloaded from WordPress.

14. Drag and drop these files to your FTP.

15. While FTP is uploading your files, go to MySQL.

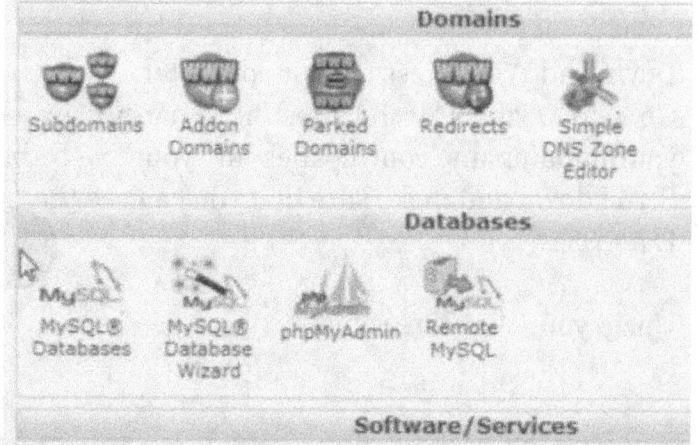

16. You can click on MySQL databases. But, it's better to click on the MySQL Database Wizard because it's easier to use.

17. Now, create a database. Enter your preferred data base name on the space next to "New Database".

18. Click on the "next step" button.

19. Enter your preferred username and then, click on the password generator to get your password. Make sure that you save your password in a safe location.

Added the database profits_db.

Step 2: Create Database Users:

Username:	profits_
	Note: seven characters max
Password:	
Password (Again):	
Strength (why?):	Very Weak (0/100)

Password Generator

20. Click on create user.

21. You'll see this page, click on "all privileges".

☑ **ALL PRIVILEGES**

☑ ALTER	☑ CREATE
☑ CREATE ROUTINE	☑ CREATE TEMPORARY TABLES
☑ CREATE VIEW	☑ DELETE
☑ DROP	☑ EXECUTE
☑ INDEX	☑ INSERT
☑ LOCK TABLES	☑ REFERENCES
☑ SELECT	☑ SHOW VIEW
☑ UPDATE	

22. Now, go back to your FTP. You'll see that your WordPress files have been uploaded.

23. It's time to start the installation process.

24. Now, type http://www.yourdomainname.com/wp_admin/install.php on your web browser. This will start the installation process.

25. Now, you'll see this page. Click on "create a configuration file". Then, click on "let's go".

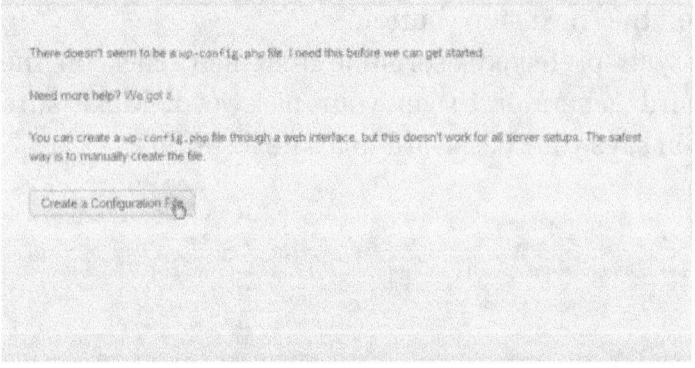

26. You'll see this page.

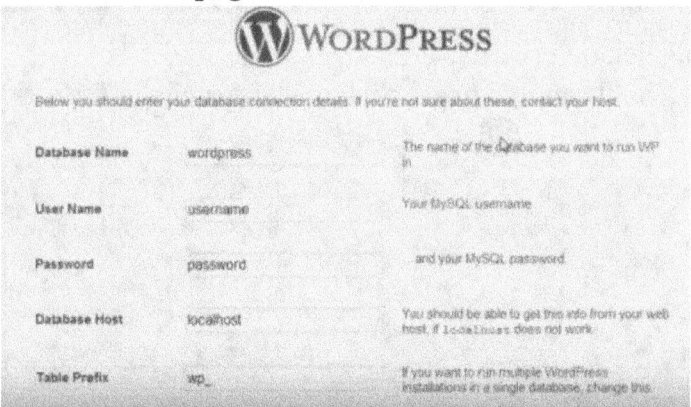

27. Now, enter your database name and your password.
28. Your database host should be local host and the table prefix should be "wp_".

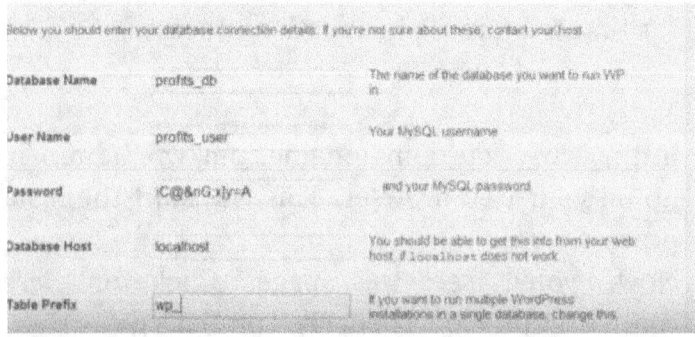

29. Click on "submit".
30. You'll see this. Copy this information.

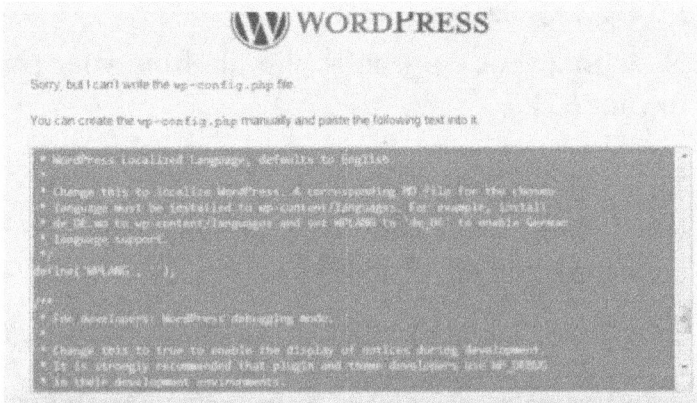

31. Then, go to your computer files and right click on wp_config.php. Click on open with Word Pad. Select all and delete.

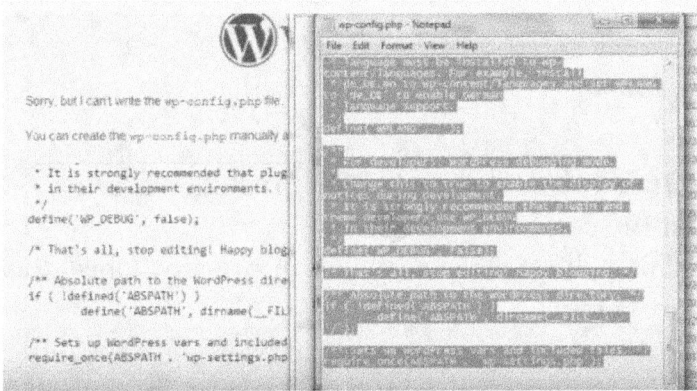

32. Now, copy everything on WP file to your wp_config.php file.

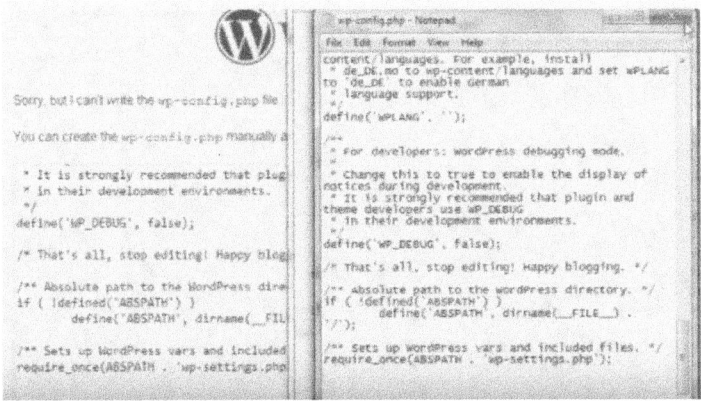

33. Click on "save".

34. Now drag your wp_config.php file from your computer to your FTP.

35. Then, click on "run install".

36. Now, enter your site title, admin name, preferred password, and email address.

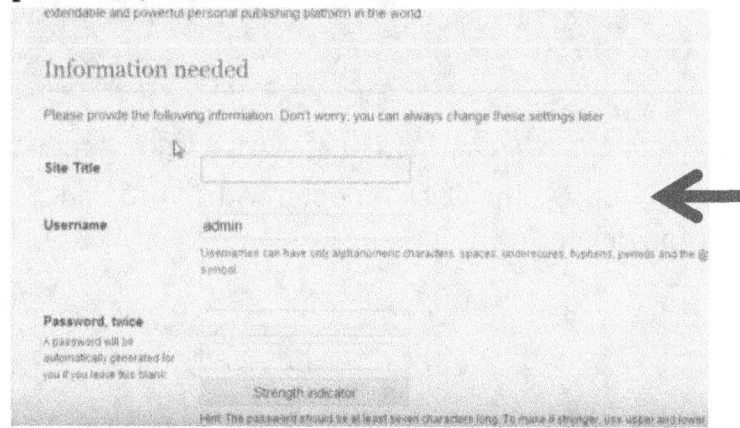

37. Once you're done, click on "Install WordPress" located at the bottom of the screen.

38. This will start the installation process. Once done, click on "log in".

39. Enter your username and password.

Now, you can start posting!

Chapter Twelve

Installing Themes – Free Themes and Theme Clubs

There are hundreds of free WordPress themes. These themes are perfect for bloggers, small business, and even e-commerce sites. These themes are incredibly responsive. This means that it looks good in any device – desktop computer, laptop, tablet, and smartphones.

But, how do you install themes? Well, it's quite easy.

1. Log in to your WordPress account.

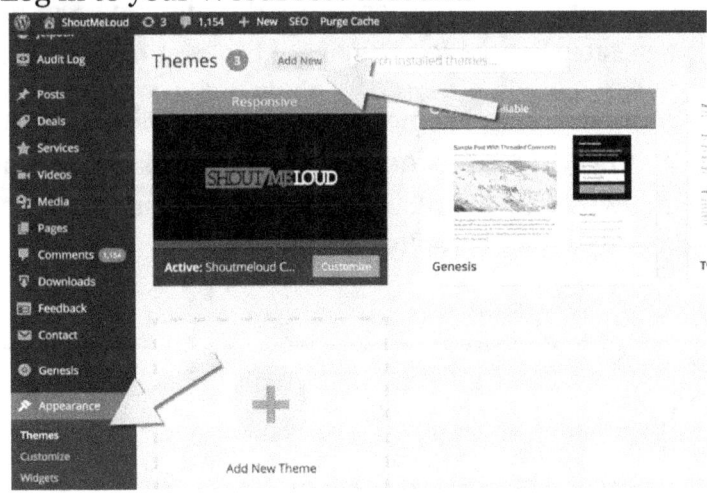

Photo Source: shoutmeloud.com

2. Go to "appearance".
3. Go to "themes".
4. Click on "add new".
5. Click on "upload theme".

6. Choose the free theme that you like. Then click on "install now".

7. You'll see this page. Click on the "preview" link to see how your site will look like with the new theme.

Photo Source: shoutmeloud.com

8. Click on "activate".

Free WordPress Themes

You do not have to break the bank to use WordPress themes. There are hundreds of themes that you can use for your WordPress site. But, here's the list of the best ones:

1. Sydney – This theme is clean and professional looking. It's best for businesses. It is translation ready. It includes social links and it allows you to add a slider header which is really cool.

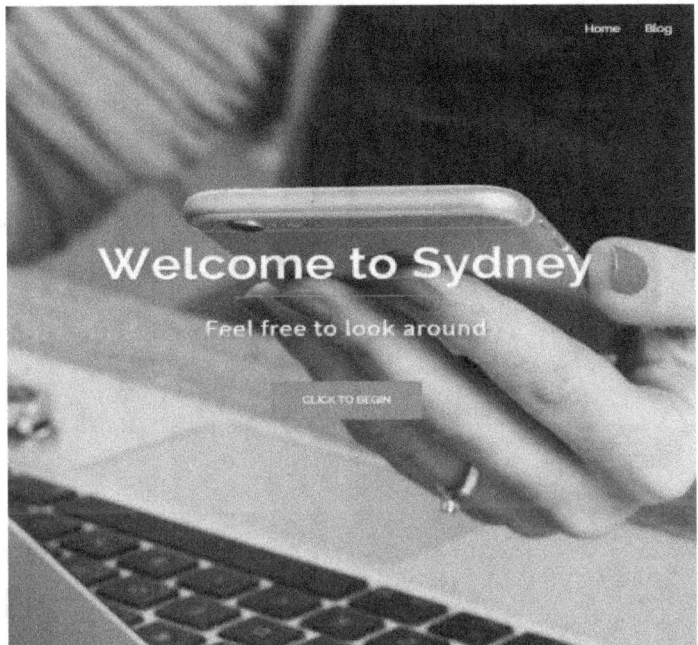

Photo Source: codeinwp.com

2. ShopIsle – This has a widgetized footer and a responsive contact form. It is also translation ready and it is WooCommerce ready. It is perfect for those who want to build an online store.

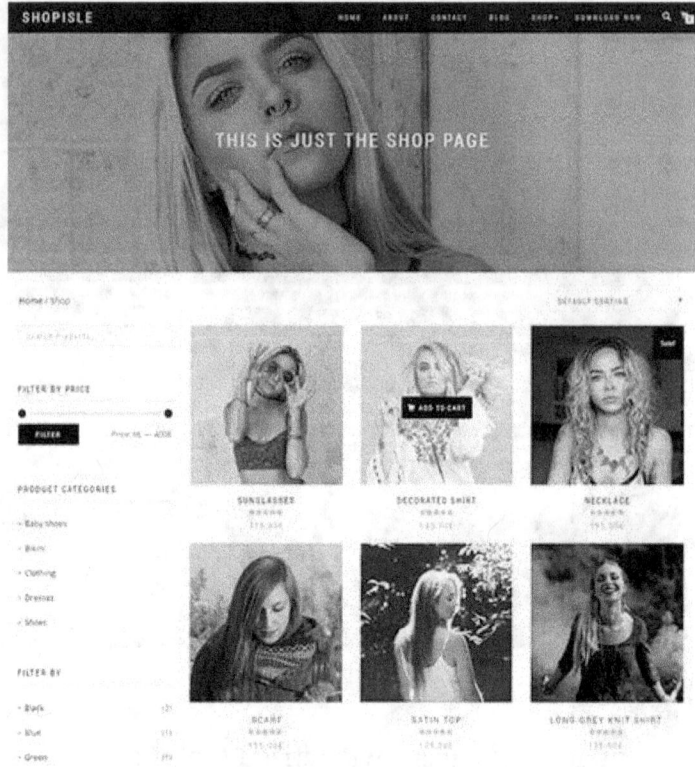

Photo Source: shopisle.com

3. Allegiant – This is an elegant theme that's perfect for all kinds of business. You can use it to showcase your portfolios. You can use it for both startups and big companies.

Photo Source: shopisle.com

4. Flash - Flash has a full width slider that has a clean and responsive design. It has color options and it comes with a flash toolkit plugin. It also has great product filters.

5. Palmas – This theme has a dainty design that's perfect for writers who want to showcase their work. It has a featured slider and it is optimized to increase site speed.

Photo Source: shopisle.com

6. ReviewZine – This theme has a responsive design. It has an attractive slider, too, and it supports several languages. It has a widgetized footer and it has an elegant, modern design.

7. Parallax One – This theme has a simple design and it has a parallax effect. It comes with attractive logos, menus, and icons.

8. OnePress – This theme has a clean and responsive design. It has a parallax effect and it supports WooCommerce.

9. Astrid – This is perfect for small business owners. If you want to showcase your portfolio, this is the perfect WP theme for you.

10. Spacious- This theme has a minimalist design. It has a responsive slider and it is compatible with WooCommerce.

11. Restaurant Theme – As the name suggests, this is perfect for restaurants.

12. Bento – This theme is perfect for graphic artists who want to showcase their designs. It has a flexible layout and it's compatible with WooCommerce.

13. Amadeus – This theme has a modern design and it is SEO-friendly. It has an elegant feel and a minimalist design.

14. Everly Lite – This theme is perfect if you plan to have SEO work done on your site. It has a responsive layout and it is widget ready.

15. Lavander Lite – This has a responsive design and it has multiple posts. It also has a minimalist design that's clean and elegant.

16. Point – This has a responsive design and it comes with custom widgets.

17. Azera Shop – This theme is perfect for online stores and even blogs. It is compatible with WooCommerce.

18. Kale – This theme has cool sliders that you can use to showcase your products.

19. Virtue – Virtue has a beautiful art gallery that's perfect for portfolios and online shops.

20. Simple – As the name suggests, this theme has a simple design. It is SEO-friendly and photo-friendly.

21. Magazine – This theme is perfect for magazine-like blogs who feature celebrity stories. It is clean and it comes with more than forty layout choices.

22. Corporate Plus – As the name suggests, this theme is perfect for corporate websites.

There are hundreds of other awesome and free themes that you can use. Just go to https://wordpress.org/themes/.

Theme Clubs

Theme clubs provide premium WP themes on membership basis. If you choose to become a member of one of these theme clubs, you'll have access to high quality WordPress themes. The membership is usually renewed every month or every year. These club offers professional quality designs and live front-end demos. They also provide customer support to members. These clubs usually offers designs for specific niches like businesses or online store.

Here's a list of the best theme clubs:

1. WooThemes
2. **Elegant Themes (Authors Best pick – Click Here To Join!)**
3. NattyWP
4. Templatic
5. StudioPress
6. Obox
7. WPZOON
8. Obox
9. Upthemes
10. Themify

Theme clubs are useful for web designers who develop multiple websites. If you plan to create just one website, it's not practical to join a theme club.

Chapter Thirteen

Adding and Editing Menu Items

One of the best things about WordPress is that you can customize almost everything about it. To increase your productivity and efficiency, WP allows you to add, remove, and edit your menu items.

To do this:

1. Log in to your WordPress using your username and password. This will take you to your dashboard.
2. Hover over "appearance" which is located at the left side of your screen.
3. Now, when you see the sub-menu, click on "menus".
4. Select the menu that you would like to edit. You may have different menus depending on how your website was designed. But, most WordPress websites have two menus – the footer menu and the main menu.
5. You'll see the menu structure. On the upper left side of your screen, you'll see the list of all the pages and services that you can add to your menu.
6. Now, click on the box next to the item that you want to add to your menu.
7. Click on the "add menu" button.
8. Now, the item is already added to the menu.
9. To edit the structure of your menu, you can just click and drag items into the place that you want to put it in.
10. You can also make an item a submenu by clicking, dragging it, and placing it below under its "parent menu item". Sub-menus are usually indented to the left.
11. To edit the menu item label, just click on the drop-down menu on the right side of the item. This allows you to

edit your navigation level. You can also click on "remove" if you wish to remove this item from the menu.

12. Once you're done editing your menu labeling and structure, click on "save menu".

Now, you have a customized and gorgeous menu!

Chapter Fourteen

Plug In Basics

One of the biggest advantages of using a self-hosted wordpress is the ability to install and use plugins. Plug ins are additional functionalities that you can add to your WordPress website.

Plugins allow you to customize and expand the functionalities of your website. These plugins allow you to add beautiful galleries, forms, calendars, SEO tools, social media sharing buttons, and more awesome stuff to your website.

There are thousands of free plugins in the <u>Word Press Plug In Directory</u> like Contact Form 7, Akismet, Yoast SEO, WooCommerce, Limit Login Attempts, and Duplicate Post. There are also a number of paid plug ins.

But, why would you want paid plugins? Well, paid plugins are usually maintained by a team of developers and support staff. These support staff can help you with compatibility issues **and also keep the security patches up to date which is very important with a Wordpress site**.

How To Install WordPress Plugin

There are three ways to install a plugin:
- ✓ Automatically install the plugin through WordPress.
- ✓ Manually upload the plugin via FTP.
- ✓ Manually upload the plugin through a medium like a server set-up.

The easiest way to install a plugin is to do it through WordPress. You can do this by following these steps:

1. Log in to your WordPress by entering your user name and password.
2. Now, go to plugins and click on the "add new" link.

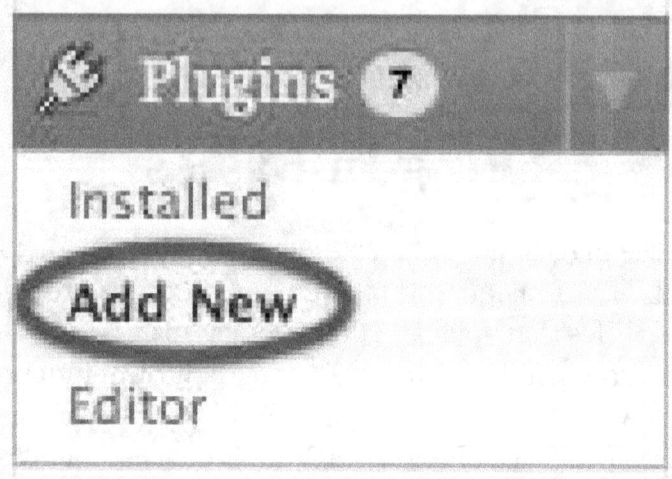

3. This will take you to the "install" screen. Now go to the "search" section and type the plugin you want to install. Click on "search plugin".

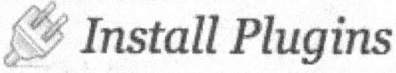

Plugins extend and expand the functionality of WordPress. or upload a plugin in .zip format via this page.

Search

Search for plugins by keyword, author, or tag.

4. You'll see this. Click on "install".

5. Once you're done, click on "activate plugin".

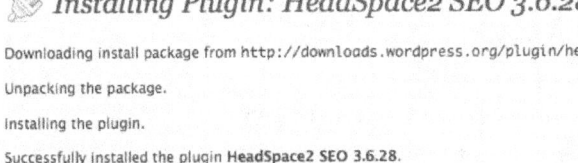

You're done! It's that simple!

Best WordPress Plugins

After WordPress was launched, hundreds (if not thousands) of web developers have created plugins that increases the functionality of a WordPress site. So, there's literally thousands of WordPress plugins, but here's the list of the best plugins that you should install in your self-hosted website.

1. **WordPress SEO by Yoast**

A good website content is nothing without enough search engine visibility. To increase the visibility of your website in the search results pages of Google or Yahoo, it's a good idea to install the WordPress SEO plugin to your website.

This plug in allows you to easily add title tags and meta tags on your posts. It is incredibly easy to use. When you are writing the meta information for your post, this plugin gives you a preview of the Google result snippet. This way, you'll see exactly how your post looks like when someone search for it on Google.

This plugin helps you create site maps that support images. It also notifies the search engines once your post is published.

It has other awesome features like:

- ✓ Focus keyword testing
- ✓ Permalink cleanups
- ✓ XML news sitemaps
- ✓ Robots.txt editor
- ✓ .htaccess editor
- ✓ Improved canonical support
- ✓ Redirects setups
- ✓ Video tutorial

2. Backup Buddy

This is a powerful plugin that helps you setup a reliable backup timetable for your site. You can use this plugin to save your content backup in multiple locations such as your computer, a cloud storage service, or an FTP server. It allows you to sleep soundly at night knowing that all your website posts are safe and backed up.

3. WPForms

Building website forms usually take time. WPForms has an easy "drag and drop" system that allows you to create contact forms, order forms, email subscriptions, and payment forms in just a few minutes.

This plugin allows you to create 100 percent responsive forms. This means that your forms look good on all types of devices – laptop, desktop computer, tablet, and mobile phones. This plugin has a number of pre-built workflows and form templates so it's definitely easy to use.

4. Disqus

This powerful commenting system is best for high traffic websites. This is a third party commenting system that does not affect your server so it does not affect your site loading speed. It also has anti-spam filters so it automatically filters out spam comments and blocks out the autobots.

5. Login Lockdown or Loginizer

To protect your site from hackers, install login lockdown to your self-hosted site. Most hackers rely on a long list of passwords to break into your website's admin area. This plugin limits the login attempts on your website. It locks down the admin area of the website for a limited time after a number of attempts.

6. OptinMonster

This plugin helps you cash in your website by converting casual website visitors into email subscribers (marketing leads). This plugin helps you to grow your email list.

7. Sucuri

Security is one of the biggest problems of online business owners. Sucuri is a plugin that protects your website from malware threats, DDOs, brute force attacks, XSS attacks, and other types of attack. It is basically a firewall that you can easily integrate into your self-hosted site through WordPress.

8. Soliloquy

Sliders are attractive and you can use to showcase your company's products. It allows you to display your products, featured content, and announcements in an interactive way. The sliders are translation ready so it's great for international audiences. It has a simple drag and drop system that makes it user friendly.

9. CSS Hero

WordPress themes are created via cascading style sheets (CSS). CSS allows you to customize the look of your website.

CSS Hero is a plugin that allows you to customize a WordPress theme without writing a code.

10. Beaver Builder

This plugin allows you to build a landing page without learning how to code. It is a drag and drop page builder tool that you can use. Aside from the Beaver Builder, you can also use a number of other drag and drop website builder plugins such as Elementor, Divi, and Themify Builder.

11. Hummingbird

People do not stay on websites for more than 8 seconds. If it takes too long for your site to load, visitors would most likely leave your site before they get to see what your site is about.

Caching can speed up your site. This is where Hummingbird comes in. This plugin scans your website and checks site issues. It allows you to check the overall speed of your site and fix some issues.

12. Edit Flow

Do you run a syndicated blog? Then, this plug in is perfect for you. EditFlow allows you to easily collaborate with your editorial team. This plugin has a lot of awesome features such as:

- Custom Status
- Calendar
- Notifications
- Editorial comments
- User groups
- Story budget

13. Floating Social Bar

If you want to increase your social media shares, this is the perfect plugin for you. This is a social media plugin that allows you to add a number of social networks.

14. AdSanity

This plugin allows you to manage your ads – the short codes and the widgets.

15. WPtouch

This plugin allows you to create a mobile version of your website. This plugin has a built-in support for mobile advertising, eCommerce, and custom content.

16. Jetpack

This plugin was created by the people who are behind the WordPress software. Jetpack strengthens the security of your website.

17. Akismet

This plugin provides a status history of each post comment so you'd know which comments are spam.

18. Redirection

This plugin helps you manage your 301 redirections and keep track of your 404 errors. Redirection automatically adds a 301 redirection whenever you change the permalink of your posts. But, you can also use this plugin to manually add 302, 307, and 301 redirections.

19. Mailchimp

Mailchimp is one of the popular email marketing services in the market today. It allows you to send emails, track results, and manage subscribers. This tool is perfect for small business owners who are trying to get more leads.

20. Envira Gallery

You can easily create beautiful galleries in WordPress. But, Envira Gallery allows you to create responsive and beautiful galleries through their user-friendly interface.

Plugins are fun, useful, easy to install, and most of them are free! These plugins allow you to save money, increase your site efficiency, improve your productivity, increase your website visibility, and maybe help you earn more revenue.

Chapter Fifteen

How to Add and Edit Pages and Posts

WordPress has a user-friendly system that allows you to easily add and edit your website pages and posts. You do not need to have a degree in computer science or web design to learn how to edit and add pages and posts.

How to Add and Edit Pages

To add and edit pages, you need to follow these steps:

1. Log in to your WordPress dashboard and then click on "content".
2. You'll see a drop-down menu, go to website pages.
3. Now, click on the "create a new website page" button.
4. Once you're done, you'll need to choose a template for your page. Go to the template menu located at the left side of your screen.
5. Choose the template that you like. Enter the page name and then, click on "create".
6. Now, below the page title, type your content.
7. Once you're done. Click on "settings" at the top center portion of your page.

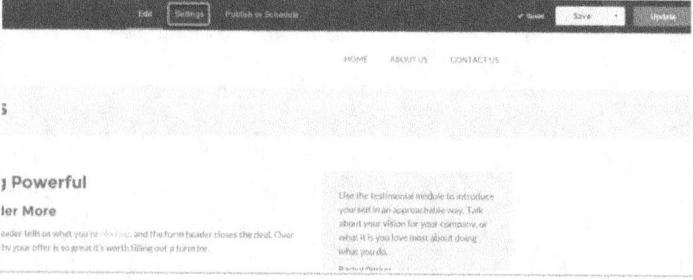

Photo Source: knowledge.hubspot.com

8. You would see this page. Type in your page name, page title, page URL, and meta description. The page name is the internal name for your page while the page title is the one that will appear on the page. The URL is the link that appears on the users' browser when they visit the page.

The meta description is the content that appears below the link in the search engine results page of Google or Yahoo. It is the description of what the page is about. We'll discuss this in detail in the later part of this book.

If you wish to run an ad campaign, click on the "select campaign" menu.

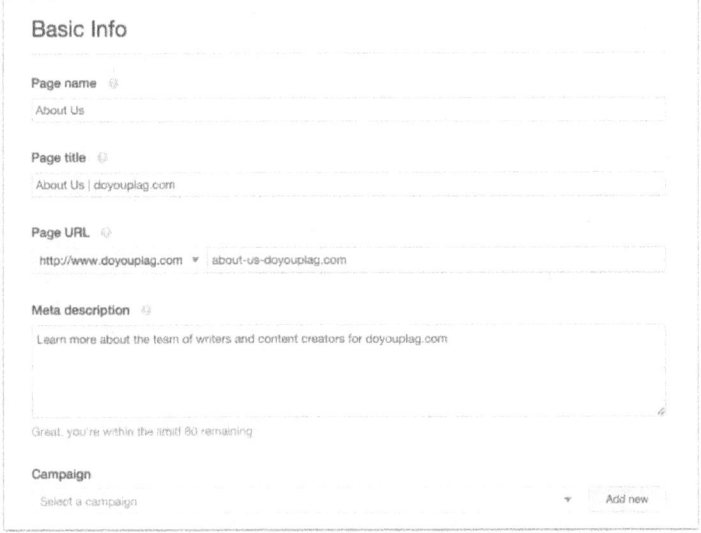

Photo Source: knowledge.hubspot.com

9. Once you're done click on save.

10. To increase your website traffic and improve your online presence, it is necessary to do SEO on your site. SEO is search engine optimization and it is the process of increasing your ranking on search results page (SRP) of the top search engines like Yahoo and Google.

To optimize your page, go to the SEO section and then, click on the "bar graph" icon.

Under the "this website page is about", type in your targeted keywords. For   example, if you sell women's shoes in New York, it's best to target the   keywords "shoes New York", "women's shoes in New York", and "New York women's shoes". The keywords are the words or phrase that potential customers   type on Google to find businesses like yours.

11. Click on the "eye" icon located at the left side of your screen. Click on "device preview" to see how your website looks like on desktop computers, laptops, smart phones, and tablets.

12. If you're satisfied with how your page looks like, click on "publish" or "schedule".

    If you wish to publish the post right away click on "publish now". If you wish to schedule the post some other time, click on the blue "schedule" button.

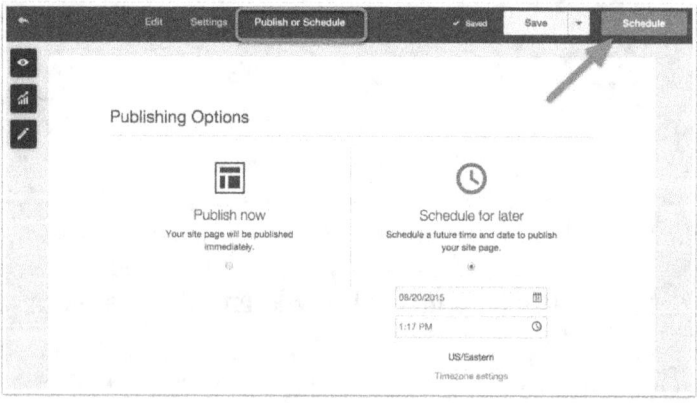

Your new website page is now ready!

How To Add and Edit Posts

Now, it's time to add a post by following these steps:

1. Go to your dashboard.
2. Now, click on "posts" located on the upper left side of your screen. A sub-menu will appear, choose all posts.
3. You'll see the list of all your posts.
4. To add a new post click on add new.
5. Enter your blog title and content.
6. Once you're done, go to the SEO section at the bottom of your page. This section will appear if you have already installed the **Yoast SEO plug in.**

Photo Source: ShoutMeLoud.com

7. Go to the left side of your screen. Add a new category. If you're writing about "yoga" for example, you can add "yoga" category.
8. Below the categories, you'll see tags. Tags make your posts searchable so make sure to add your "keyword" as your post tag. For example, if you're a chiropractor in San Francisco writing about the benefits of going to a chiropractor, you may want to add relevant tags such as "chiropractor" or "alternative medicine".

Photo Source: siteground.com

9. Click on edit next to your permalink – the link to your site. You want to keep this short and relevant to your post.

Photo Source: ithemes.com

10. Click on "preview" to see how your site looks like.

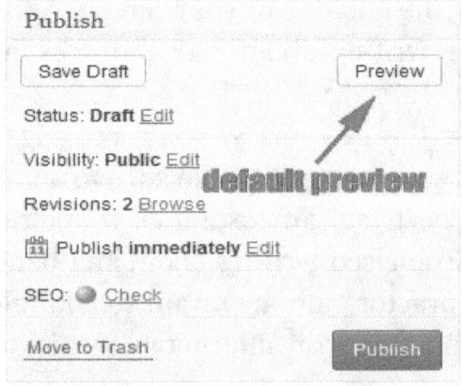

Photo Source: WPsamurai.ph

11. If you're satisfied with how your site looks like, click on the blue "publish" button.

Now, if you wish to edit your post, follow these steps:

1. Click on "posts" located at the right side of your screen.
2. A sub-menu will appear, click on "all posts".
3. You'll see all your posts.

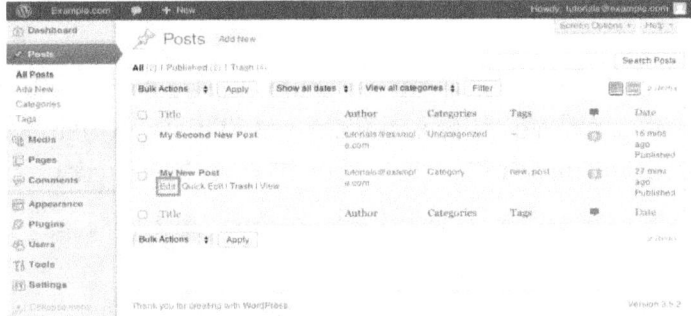

Photo Source: HostMonsteraccount.com

4. Click on "edit" below the title of the post you want to edit.
5. Edit your post.
6. Once you're done, click on the "preview changes" button.

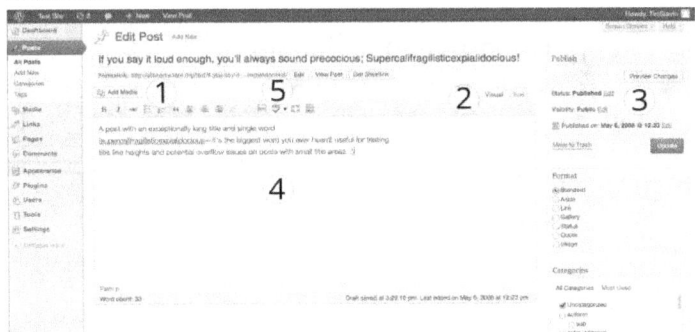

Photo Source: kidscodecs.com

7. If you're satisfied with the changes, click on the blue "update" button at the right part of your screen.

Your post is now updated!

Chapter Sixteen

Use the Screen Options Menu At the Top

The screen options is a menu that's located at the top right corner of your WordPress dashboard. This will help you add extra stuff in the admin area of your WordPress account.

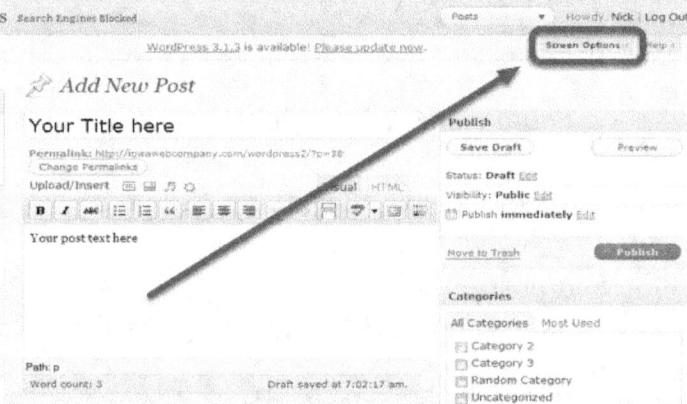

Your screen option should look like this:

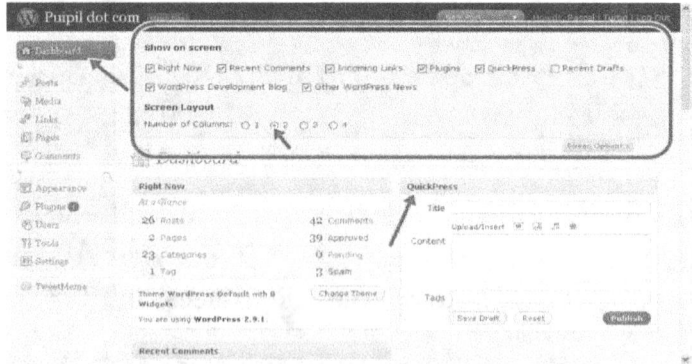

Photo Source: fourblogger.com

There's a lot of search options. You just have to click the ones that are useful for you. Then, click on apply.

Chapter Seventeen

How To Create A Page Dedicated to Blog Posts

WordPress supports a popular blogging system that top bloggers use. But, if you use your website for different purposes like e-commerce, portfolio showcase, and blogging, you may want to create a separate page for your blog posts.

You can do so by following these steps:

1. Go to your dashboard.
2. Click on "pages" at the left side of your screen.
3. A sub-menu will appear, click on "add new".
4. Under title, type in "Blog".
5. Now, go to the template located at the right side of your screen. Choose a template that you like or you can always go with "default template" which comes with your theme.
6. The comments are automatically enabled, but if you want to disable it just uncheck the "enable comments" box.
7. Click on publish.
8. Now, you need to separate your blog page from the rest of your website pages.
9. Click on settings. You'll see the "reading settings" page.

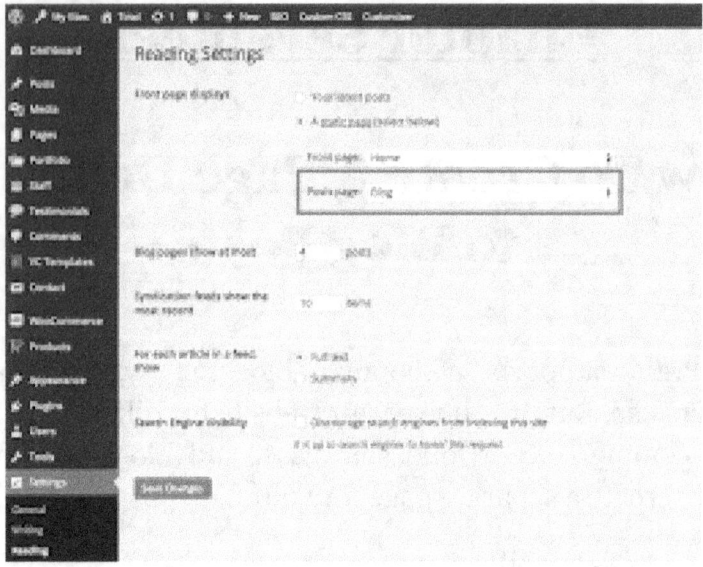

10. Under the front page, choose "home".

11. Then, under posts page, choose blog.

12. Enter how many blog pages you want to show on your website.

13. Click on "full text" to display the full text of each post.

14. Now, click on "save changes".

Separating your blog from the other sections makes it easier for your visitors to navigate your site. This allows them to easily locate your blog from your home page. It also gives your website a much more polished look.

Chapter Eighteen

Static HomePage or Blog Posts? How To Change The Setting

A WordPress website can have a static or dynamic home page and blog posts. By default, WordPress displays your latest posts on your home page. This is called the "dynamic home page". Some website owners prefer what we call a "static home page". This is a custom home page that does not feature your latest posts. This is particularly useful for people who wants to separate their blog from their website. But, why would you want to separate your blog posts from your website?

Well, for one, separating your blog posts from the other pages in your site makes your website look more professional. The static home page is usually used by businesses as it allows them to showcase their products instead of their blog posts.

First, you need to create a home page following the process outlined in chapter 15. Then, click on "reading" at the left side of the screen.

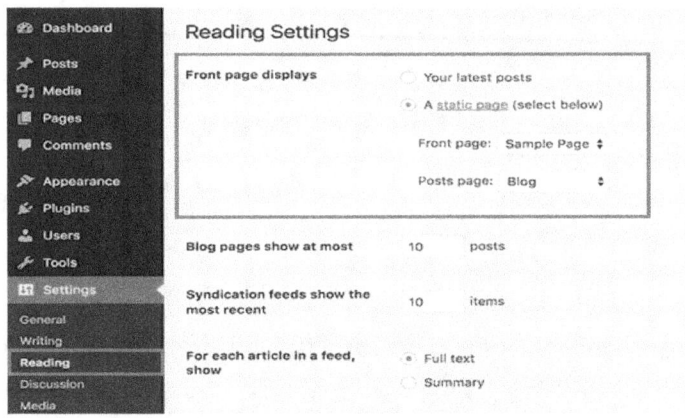

Photo Source: wpbeginner.com

Click on the "static page" radio button. Then, enter "home page" next to "front page". Save changes and you're done.

Remember that any WP page can be used as a "static front page". But, you need to publish a page first before you can use it as a static front page.

Chapter Nineteen

How To Allow and Disallow Comments

Placing a comment section on your posts allow your readers and customers to give you feedback. But, spammers also use these section to post malicious links. If you're trying to grow your business and connect with your customers, it's best to allow comments on your posts, by following these steps.

1. Log in to your WordPress account.
2. Go to settings.
3. Then, click on the discussion tab.
4. Go to default settings and make sure that the "allow people to post comments on new articles" box is ticked. Don't tick it if you want to disallow comments on your posts.

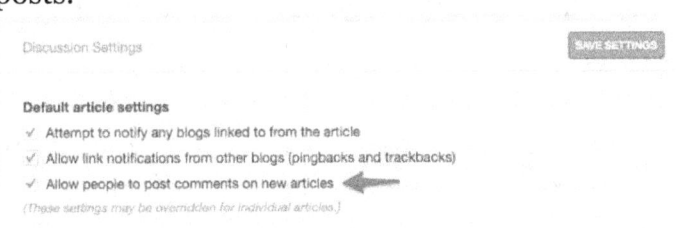

Photo Source: en.support.wordpress.com

Then, click on "save settings".

If you're running a blog, it may be a good idea to allow comments so you can engage with your audience and encourage them to give a feedback. But, if you're running a business website, it's probably best to disable the comments section on your pages. This makes your website look more business-like and professional.

Chapter Twenty

How To Add Media and Edit Images in Your Media Folders Using WordPress Images Editor

Photos and videos add visual value to your website. But, before you add photos and videos to your website, you must follow these rules:

1. Add photos and videos that are related to the content of your site.
2. Add photos that are compatible with your site design.
3. Make sure to use uncopyrighted images and videos. Always include your source.
4. Try to use original photos as much as you can.
5. Make sure that the image that you use are clear.

Add Images

To add media to your post, click on "add media" which is located at the top left corner of your post toolbar.

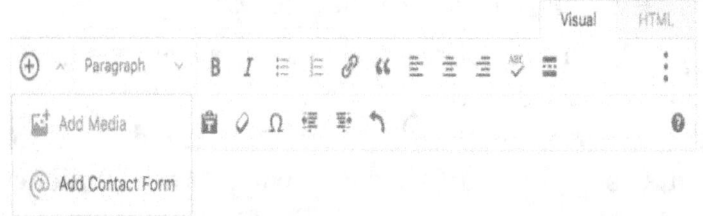

Photo Source: en.support.wordpress.com

Click on "add new". You can also click on "add via URL" if your image is displayed on another website.

Upload the photos that you want to include in your website. Then, click on the photos that you want to insert to your post. Click on "continue".

Photo Source: en.support.wordpress.com

Go to the "layout" and then choose the photos layout you want. If you're going to use multiple photos, it's best to make a collage. To do so, click on multiple photos, go to "layout" then click on either "tiled mosaic" or "square tiles".

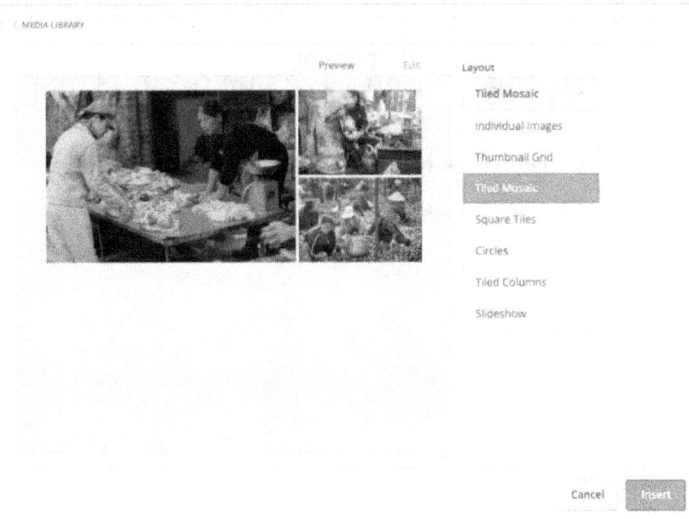

Photo Source: en.support.wordpress.com

Click on the "insert" button to insert the photos to your post.

Edit Images

Yes, there are a lot of amazing photo editing software. But, you can edit your images in WordPress, too, by following these steps:

1. Go to "add media".
2. Click on "add new" and then, upload the photo you want to edit.
3. Click on the photo that you want to edit and a pop up will appear. Click on the "edit image" button located at the lower left side of the pop up.

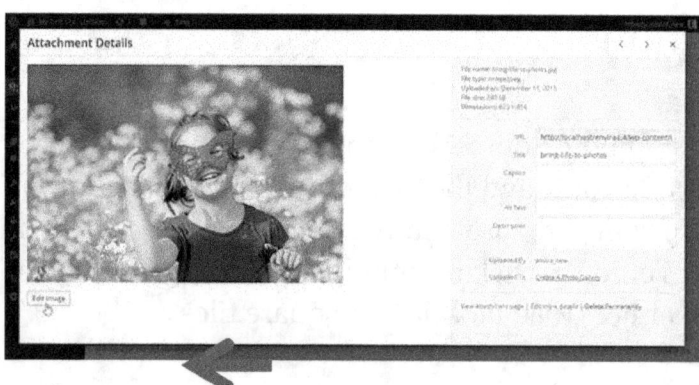

4. You'll see a menu with basic photo editing options like rotate, flip, and crop.
5. Use these buttons to edit your images.
6. Once you're done, click on save.

It's that easy!

Add Video

If you are a life coach or a fitness coach, adding a video on your website will help you introduce yourself to your potential clients.

To add a video to your post, upload your video in your YouTube channel. You can embed most videos in YouTube, just make sure to give credit where credit is due.

Go to the bottom part of the video and click on "share". Now, you'll see the link of the video. Copy that link and then, go to the Wordpress admin panel of your website.

Go to "posts" located at the left side of your screen. Then, click on "add new". Enter the title of the post. **Go to the text editor tab and click "paste". Now click on the icon below so the video does not appear as a "clickable link".**

Photo Source: agentWP.com

Then, click on save and publish. You're done!

Add Audio

To add an audio file to your self-hosted WordPress website, you need to install and activate a plugin called "oEmbed HTML5 audio".

After you activate the plugin, go to "posts" and click on "add new". Now, click on "add media" to upload the audio file from your computer. You can only upload wav, mp3, and ogg formats. Once you have uploaded the file, copy the file location.

Photo Source: wpbeginner.com

Then, paste the URL on your post. The plugin will automatically use an HTML5 audio tag to embed the file to your post. Click on "save" and "publish".

People these days have short attention spans and they do not have the time to read your blog posts. This is the reason why adding media to your posts will help hook your readers and increase your site traffic.

<u>Chapter Twenty One</u>

Adding Meta Tags to Posts

Meta tags are the description that you'll see below your URL at the search engine results page of Yahoo, Google, or any other search engine.

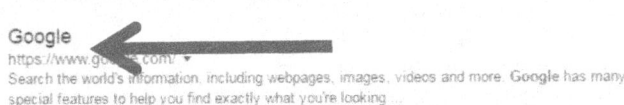

Meta can act as a "click bait". So, it is important to write a meta tag that aptly describes your business or organization. If you strategically place "keywords" on your meta tags, it can help improve your website visibility, too, and increases your website rank on the search engine results page. This means that when a person types your targeted keyword on Google, they'll instantly see your website.

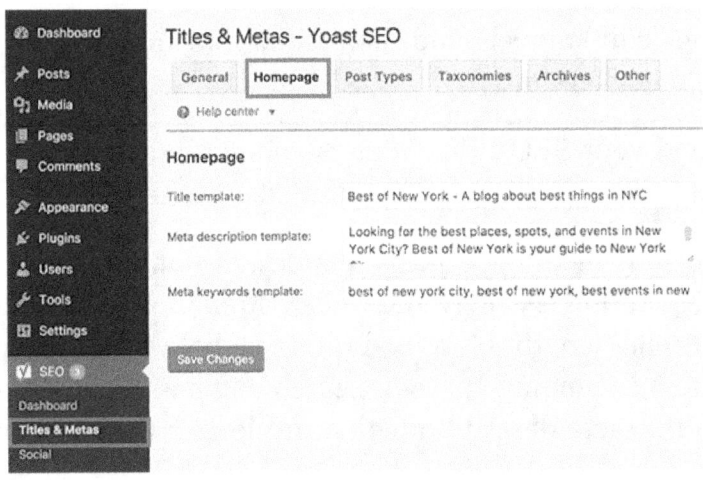

Photo Source: wpbeginner.com

To edit the meta tag of your posts or pages, make sure that you installed Yoast SEO. Then, go to the Yoast SEO section at the bottom of your post. You can also click on the Yoast SEO button located at the left side of your screen.

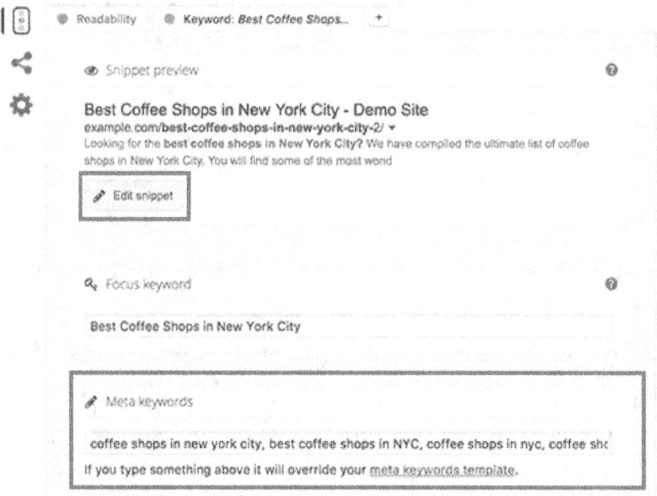

Photo Source: wpbeginner.com

Click on "edit snippet" and then enter your targeted keywords under "meta keywords".

Now, add your SEO title – this is your title tag. Make sure to place your keywords on both your meta tag and title tag.

Type in your meta tag under meta description. Make sure that your description is catchy and well-written. Also, take note that the optimal length of a meta tag is between 130 to 160 characters (including spaces). Search engines usually crop out posts with meta descriptions that are longer than the optimal length.

SEO title

Editor's Pick of The Best Coffee Shops in New York City

Slug

best-coffee-shops-in-new-york-city

Meta description

Are you looking for the best coffee shops in New York City? We have hand-picked some of the best coffee shops in New York City for you to visit.

Close snippet editor

Now, click on save changes.

<u>Chapter Twenty Two</u>

Customizing Your Sidebar in the Widgets Section

Widgets are small programs that you can install on your blog or website. They can benefit your websites in many ways. You can use them to track web visitors, provide an interactive experience to your site visitors, and display ads on your site.

But, how do you use widgets and customize your widget sidebars? Well, to use the widgets feature, you'll have to follow these steps:

1. Go to "appearance".
2. Go to "widgets".
3. Choose a widget and drag it to your sidebar. You can place it wherever you wish.
4. Once you're done, WP automatically updates your theme.
5. Now, preview your site and make sure that the widget is in the right place.
6. Go back to the "widges" section to add more widgets.
7. You can simply arrange the widgets by dragging them around.
8. You can customize the widget by clicking on the arrow next to it to expand its interface.
9. Click on "save".
10. If you want to remove it, you can simply click on "delete" or "remove".

To customize your sidebars:

1. Go to "theme settings".
2. Then, go to "general settings" and then, click on "custom sidebars".
3. Write down the alias for your sidebar, e.g. contact us, FAQ, etc.
4. Click add more aliases if you wish to add new alias names.
5. When you're done, click on "save".
6. Go to "appearance" and then click on "widgets".
7. You will now see the list of custom sidebars.
8. You can just drag and drop the widgets into your custom side bar.
9. Now, assign the custom side bar to a post by clicking on "add new page", go to "page layout", and then, "choose sidebar".
10. Choose the custom side bar from the select options.

Now, you're done!

<u>Chapter Twenty Three</u>

How to Check Your Site's Raw Analytics from cPanel in your Hosting Account

Your WordPress self-hosted website comes with raw analytics that contain important data about your website like site traffic. You can access this data by following these steps:

1. Login to cPanel.
2. Now, go to the "metrics" section.
3. Click on "raw access".

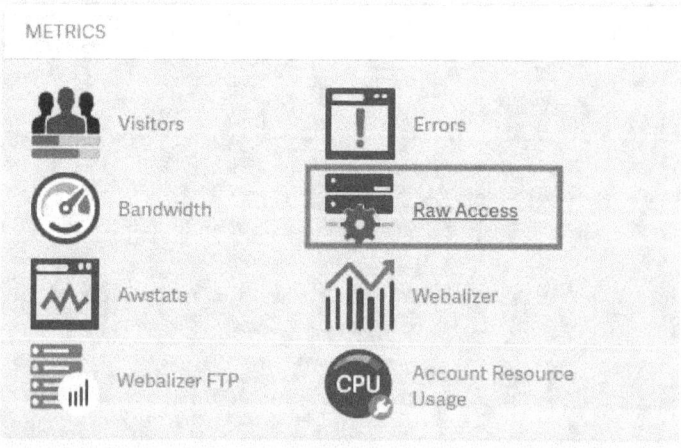

4. You will see "download current access logs". You'll see the list of the domain names in your hosting account. Select the domain you want to view statistics for.
5. Your browser will begin downloading your compressed access log.

6. Once the download is complete, uncompress the file and open it.

There's another way to view your website traffic and that's through Google Analytics which we will discuss in the next chapter.

<u>Chapter Twenty Four</u>

How To Add Tracking Codes to Your WordPress Site Using A Free Plugin

Google Analytics is a free reporting service that you can use for the marketing campaign of your business. It provides extensive data that includes your website traffic and the profile and location of your site visitors. This information is useful if you plan to run a Google or Facebook ad.

Google Analytics allows you to identify what people are searching for in your site. It also helps to detect your best and worst performing posts. So, you'll know what kind of content your customer wants.

But, to install Google Analytics, you need to add a tracking code to your site with a plug in. To do this, you'll need access to your site's FTP. You'll also need a live WordPress installation running on your theme and a code/text editor like Filezilla.

1. Check your theme's "header.php" file to make sure that you have the "wp_head" hook.
   Your plugins will insert a code to your website by attaching a code to a hook called "wp_head". This hook is used to insert styles, scripts, and more.
   To check if you have a "wp_head", go to your FTP. Open your wp-content file. Now, choose the folder that contains your themes, the folder usually starts with wp-content/themes/. Now, open a file called header.php.

You will find the wp_head hook at the bottom of the <head> section of your file.

If your head.php file does not contain the hook, add the code w_head before </head>.

2. Get your Google analytics code.

Go to https://analytics.google.com and click on sign up. This will take you to the new account page. Fill out that form.

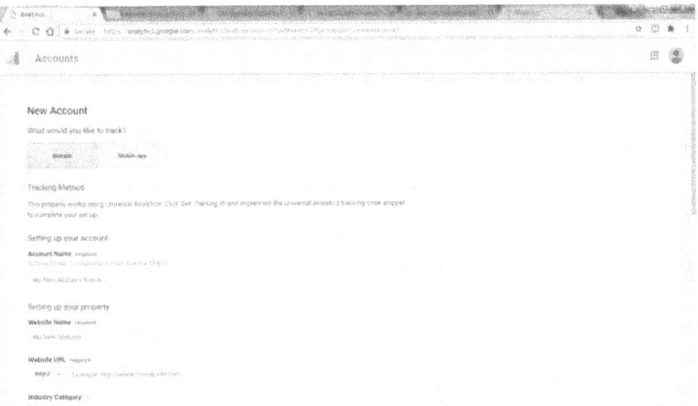

Then click on "get tracking ID".

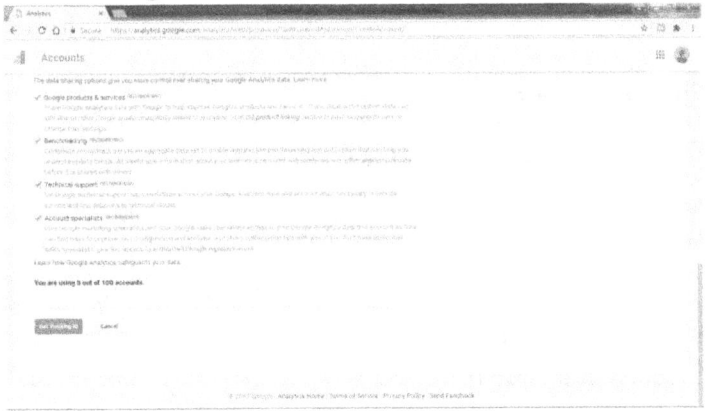

You'll get your tracking code. Copy everything from <script> and </script>

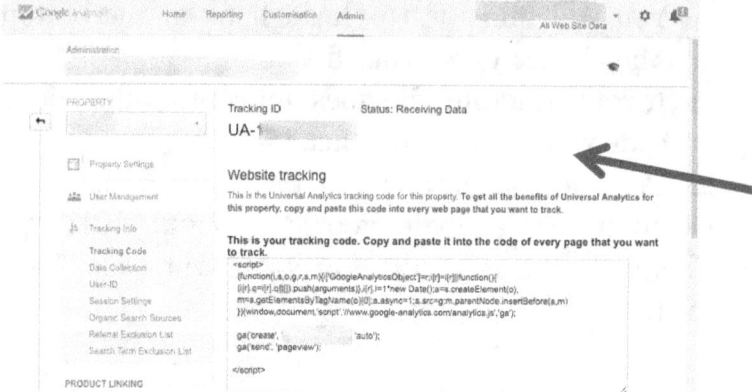

3. Create the plugin.

Now it's time to create the plugin where you add the tracking code to. Go to your wp-content/plugins folder. Click on "create a new PHP file" and name it something like wpmudev-analytics.php.

Open that file using your code editor. Now, add this code:

```php
<?php
/*
Plugin Name: Simple Google Analytics Plugin
Plugin URI: http://yourdomainname.com
Description: Adds a Google analytics tracking code to the <head> of your theme
Author: Your Name
Version: 1.0
*/
?>
```

Then, this code:

```php
<?php
function wpmudev_analytics ( ) { ?>

<?php }
add_action( 'wp_head', 'wpmudev_analytics', 10 );
```

This attaches your analytics to the hook. Now, it's time to activate your plugin.

4. Activate your plug in.

Now, let's say that this is your Google analytics tracking code:

<script type = "text/javascript">

var _gaq = _gaq II [];

```
_gaq.push(_setaccount', PA-XXX');

_gaq.push (_trackpageview);

(function() {

var = document.createelement ('script'); ga type =
"text/javascript"; ga.sync =true

ga.src = ('https:' = document.location.protocol?
'https://ssl':

</script>
```

Copy the tracking code to function script so it looks like this:

```
<?php
function wpmudev_analytics ( ) { ?>

    <script type = "text/javascript">

        var _gaq = _gaq II [];

        _gaq.push(_setaccount', PA-XXX');

        _gaq.push (_trackpageview);

        (function() {

        var = document.createelement ('script'); ga type
= "text/javascript";          ga.sync =true

        ga.src = ('https:' = document.location.protocol?
'https://ssl':

    </script>

<?php }
```

add_action('wp_head', 'wpmudev_analytics', 10)

Now, save your plug-in file. Go to your site admin page and go to "plugins". You should see your new plugin. Click on "network activate" to activate your plugin.

Wait for a few hours or a few days before Google picks up your tracking code.

Chapter Twenty Five

Set Up Traffic Analytics Using JetPack

You can also set up traffic analytics by using **JetPack**. When you log in to your WordPress dashboard, you'll see Jetpack at the center portion of your screen. But what is it? Well, it's a collection of plugins. It has a number of functionalities. It allows you to access reports, build a contact form, add a comment section to your posts, and allow visitors to subscribe to your blog.

First, you need to login to your WordPress account. Then, go to plugins. Search for "Jetpack 4.6". As of writing, this is the latest version of the plugin. This plugin is compatible with PHP 7.1 and it allows Google Analytics integration.

Click on "install now" and then, click on "activate plugin". The good news is that WordPress stats is automatically enabled when you activate Jetpack. To manually activate it, just go to your dashboard. Then, go to "screen options" and then, check the box beside site stats.

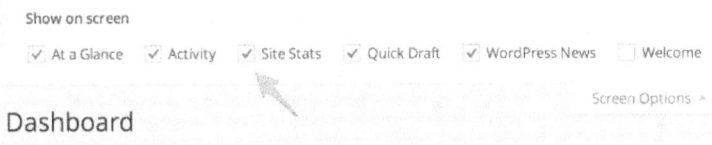

Photo Source: jetpack.com

You'll then see your site traffic stats on your dashboard.

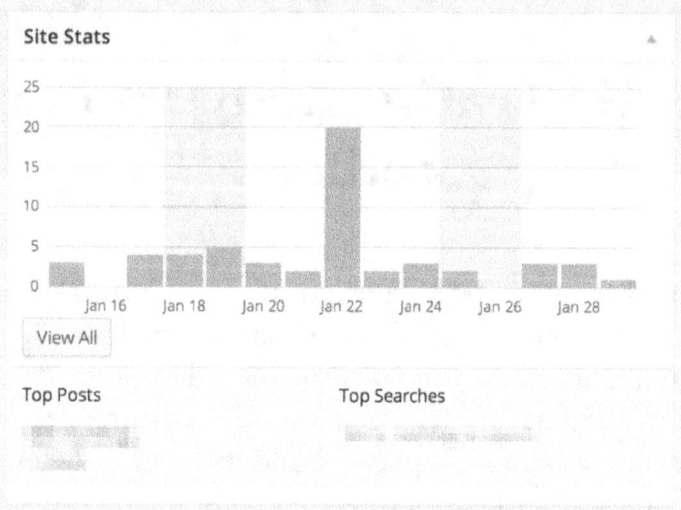

Photo Source: jetpack.com

If you want to check your top performing posts and pages, go to "view old stats". If you want to see more details about your visitors, click on "view more stats on WordPress.com)". This allows you to check the location of your visitors.

The good news is that you can use your WordPress.com stats with Google Analytics. If you have installed Jetpack, you can simply go to your dashboard. Then, go to "Jetpack". Go to "settings", then "traffic". Then, go to "Google analytics". Now, go   to https://analytics.google.com/analytics/web/provision/?authus er=0#provision/SignUp/ to sign up for a new account. Fill out the form. Then, copy the tracking code.

General   Writing   Discussion   **Analytics**   SEO   Import   Export

Analytics Settings   SAVE SETTINGS

Google Analytics Tracking ID

UA-90363941-1

Where can I find my Tracking ID?

Google Analytics is a free service that complements our built-in stats with different insights into your traffic. WordPress.com stats and Google Analytics use different methods to identify and track activity on your site, so they will normally show slightly different totals for your visits, views, etc.

Learn more about using Google Analytics with WordPress.com.

Photo Source: jetpack.com

Then, click on save settings. Wait for a few hours or a few days to view your analytics data.

Chapter Twenty Six

How to Set Up Your Domain Email Account in cPanel

Using your own domain name email adds credibility to your business. It strengthens your brand and it helps build customer trust. This also gives you maximum momentum.

You can create your own domain email account by following these steps:

1. Go to your "cPanel".
2. Then, click on "email accounts" located in the email section.
3. Enter the details of your new email account. Then, click on "create account".
4. Then, you'll get a notification that the account has already been created.
5. Now, go back to your cPanel dashboard. Go to the mail section. Click on "forwarders".
6. Fill out the form.

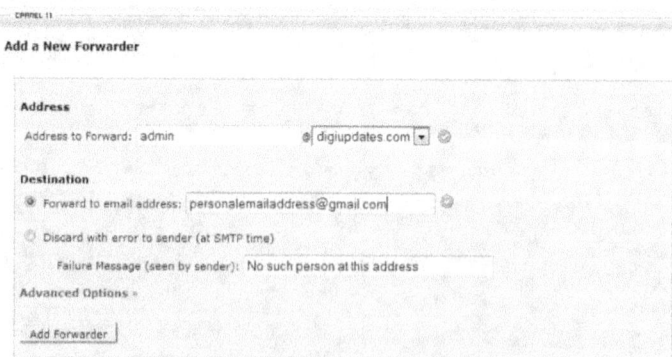

Photo Source: problogger.com

7. Click "add forwarder".
8. Now, integrate your new domain email with your Gmail.
9. Sign in to Gmail.
10. Go to options.
11. Click on mail settings.
12. Click on "accounts and imports".
13. Check "send mail as".
14. Then, click on "add another email address you own".
15. A pop up will appear. Enter the domain name that you just created.
16. Click on "next".
17. Click on "send verification".
18. Check your email inbox to see the verification email.
19. You can send a sample email to see that the changes were complete.

Conclusion

I hope that this book was able to help set up your self-hosted WordPress website or at the very least give you a better understanding of how to set up your own wordpress hosted domain with full 100% control. Having a WP site is truly useful for bloggers and small business owners. Wordpress is a great web application to help launch your business or blogging career without having to learn website coding or technology upfront.

But, remember these tips:

- ✓ Purchase a domain name that represents your brand or business.
- ✓ If you have the extra budget, you may want to also purchase the extensions associated to your .com domain such as the .net, .co, .biz, and .org. This will help protect your brand from scrupulous people who want to ride on your brand's popularity and credibility.
- ✓ Do not give your "account management panel" username and password to your web developer as this contains your billing and credit card information.
- ✓ If you are aiming to build a high traffic website, it's best to go for VPS(virtual private server) hosting. But, if you're on a budget then you may want to go for shared hosting. Remember, Wordpress does use a good amount of memory because of it operates on a database structure, your pages are dynamic not static, theres more work going on versus a plain static html website.
- ✓ Use plugins to increase your website functionality but don't overload your site with too many plugins unless you have LOTS of memory and space. Plugins should be kept at bare minimums.

✓ Invest in SSL certificate if you're running an online shop. This helps protect your customer information. This also increases your site's credibility and protection. Most good web hosting companies are offering a free SSL with a new account. Only use 3rd party verified SSL certificates, they are the most trusted. Self-signed certificates do not fully authenticate.

Finally, if you enjoyed this book, then I'd like to ask you for a favor, would you be kind enough to leave a review for this book on Amazon? It'd be greatly appreciated!

And we're not done yet! Scroll down to access the bonus section of this book!

Thank you and good luck!

Bonus Section: Secret Tips I Wish Someone Told Me When I Started WordPress

Yes, we are not done yet! There's more. When I started my first WordPress website, there's a lot of things that I didn't know. Here's a list of the things that I wish I knew before I used WordPress. I outlined them for you, so you won't commit the same mistakes that I did when I launched my first self-hosted WP website.

Buy A Verified SSL Certificate

If you're running an online store, you want to make sure that you build a safe and secure website environment for your customers. So, it's a good idea to get web security. The internet is generally good as it gives you access to truckloads of information. It also allows you to connect with people all over the world. But, the internet is filled with bad people, too.

In fact, there are a number of people who would try to steal your customer's important information like credit card numbers, pins, and social security numbers. If customers don't feel safe in your site, they won't buy the products that you're selling. So, you need to secure your website using an SSL certification.

Have you noticed that some websites begin with "https". This means that the website has what we call SSL security.

SSL is the acronym for Secure Socket Layer. It is a technology that secures sensitive data like passwords and credit cards by encrypting this information while it passes through the server. So, it can't be intercepted.

If you have an SSL certificate, you are telling your visitors that your website is secure. An SSL certificate is also a proof that you are the legitimate owner of your website. So, in a way, it increases your website's and business' credibility.

You can purchase your SSL certificate from the following providers (we recommend COMODO)

- ✓ Digicert – Digicert is used by the top websites such as Facebook, Amazon, NASA, Yahoo, and Wikipedia.

- ✓ VeriSign – If you want maximum security, you should go for VeriSign as they can do up to 256 bit encryption. But, they are a bit expensive.

- ✓ GeoTrust – Offers basic encryption for $299.

- ✓ **Comodo** – Offers SSL certificates for just about anybody – from blogs to e-commerce websites.

- ✓ GoDaddy –GoDadddy is the biggest domain registration site. They also offer SSL certificates.

Best Tip: Get the "Duplicate Page" Plugin To Quicly Churn Out Templated Web Pages In WordPress.

You want consistency in your web design so sometimes, you use template webpages to achieve this.

Duplicate Page is a plugin that you can use to duplicate your pages and posts in just one click. You just need to install this plugin. Then, activate it. Go to "Duplicate Page Settings" from the settings tab. Then go to "Create New Post/Page". Then, after typing your content, you'll see the "duplicate this post/draft" option.

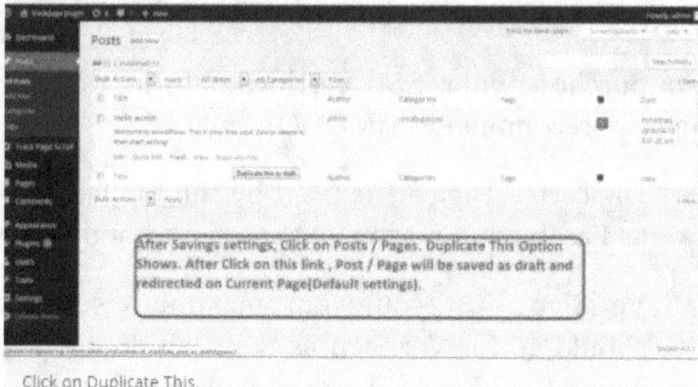

Click on Duplicate This.

Click on that and voila! You'll see the duplicate of your post.

Security Tips

Your website serves as the online "front desk" of your business. So, it has to be secured. Here's a list of top security tips that can protect your website from attackers:

1. Use strong passwords.

We all know that we are supposed to use strong passwords. But, we end up using a password that's easy to remember and easy to hack. To protect your website from hackers, you have to follow these tips:

- ✓ Use a unique password for **each account**.
- ✓ Do not use your name, birthday, or other personal information as your password.
- ✓ Make sure that your backup password information and options are updated.

2. Use HTTPS.

Getting an SSL certificate is one of the best things that you can do for your website.

3. Install a security plugin.

Install a security plugin to keep your site safe from malware and brute-force attacks. Here's a list of the best WordPress security plugins that you can use:

- ✓ Sucuri Security – This offers continuous malware scanning. It stops DDoS attacks and hacks immediately. It also provides help for hacked websites.
- ✓ Jetpack – This plugin protects your website from brute-force attacks from hackers and botnets. It also notifies your site whenever you have a downtime.
- ✓ WPS Hide Login – This is a simple plugin that prevents brute force attack.
- ✓ **All In One WP Security & Firewall** – This plugin has a password strength tool that helps you and your site visitors create strong passwords. It also has a one-click database backup. It also includes a firewall that protects against XSS or Cross Site Scripting.
- ✓ Shield Security – This plugin blocks suspicious URLs. It also provides security against brute force attacks.
- ✓ Updraft Plus – This enables you to backup your website and upload it to cloud service providers like Google Drive and Dropbox.

4. Tighten the network security of your website.

If your website is maintained by various people in your office, you need to tighten your network security. You have to ensure that passwords are changed frequently and that logins expire after a short period of time.

5. Hide your admin page.

Use robot_txt file to discourage Google from listing your site admin page.

Your website represents your brand and your company. So, you must make security a priority.

How to Remove or Change The Theme Author Name At Footer Using The HTML Editor Option

There are two ways to change the theme author name at the footer. You can change it through CSS or you can do it through an HTML text editor. But, you should avoid the CSS method at all cost as it's going to mess up your site SEO.

To change the theme author name through your HTML text editor, you should follow these steps:

1. Log in to your WordPress dashboard and then click on the "editor"

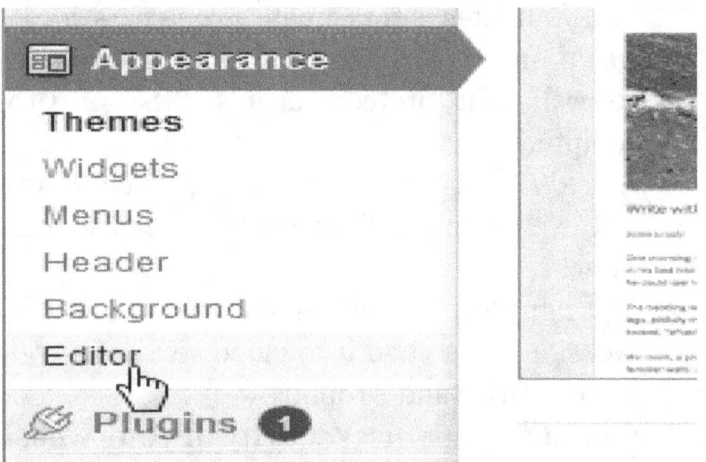

Photo Source: inmotionhosting.com

2. Now, click on "Footer" to edit your footer.php link.

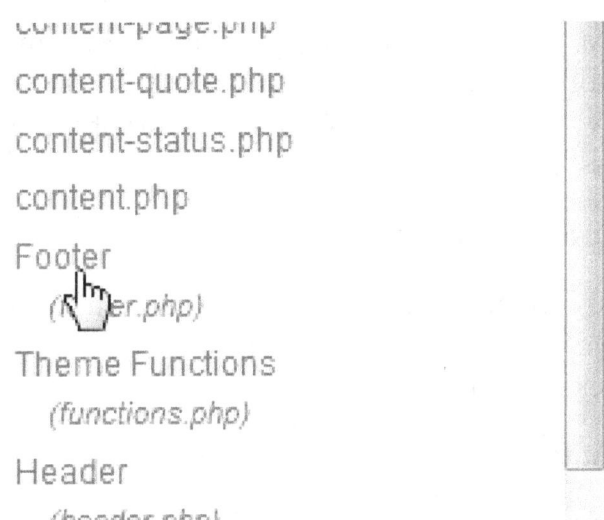

content-quote.php

content-status.php

content.php

Footer

(footer.php)

Theme Functions

(functions.php)

Header

(header.php)

3. Find the code that shows the text at the bottom. Which looks like the highlighted text:

<div class="site-info">

  <?php

   /**

    * Fires before the footer text for footer customization.

    *

    */

   do_action

  ?>

   <span class="site-title"><a href="<?php echo esc_url(home_url('/')); ?>" rel="home"><?php bloginfo('name'); ?></a></span>

```
<a      href="<?php     echo      esc_url(      __(
'https://wordpress.org/',  'twentysixteen'  )  );  ?>"><?php
printf( __( 'Proudly powered by %s',     'twentysixteen'     ),
'WordPress' ); ?></a>

</div><!-- .site-info -->
```

You can either change it to your company name or you can remove it.

4. Click on update.

Add The Auto Legal Pages Plug In

Legal pages increases your website credibility. Search engines like Google also prefer to index websites with legal pages. So, it is best to add auto legal pages plug in such as the "WP Legal Pages". This plugin includes privacy policy, DCMA policy, and EU cookie policy. The premium version of this plug in includes:

✓ Linking policy
✓ Facebook privacy policy
✓ Cookie policy template
✓ Anti-spam policy
✓ Terms and conditions
✓ Affiliate agreement
✓ Refund policy

The pages that you create using this plug in are easy to edit and modify. The plug in also has a force agreement option. This means that you can force your users to agree to the terms.

This plug in is easy to use and the free option is already packed. So, you won't have to upgrade to the premium version.

How to Retrieve Your WordPress Web Login PassWord From Your Back-End Hosting Account in PHP MyAdmin – A Life Saver

If you don't update your website frequently, you'll most likely forget your password. But, the good news is, you can retrieve or reset your password using PHP MyAdmin by following these steps:

1. Log in to your server admin account. It can be through Hsphere, Plesk, or cPanel.
2. Open your PHP MyAdmin.
3. Then, go to your WebPress database.
4. Click on wp_users at the left side of the screen.

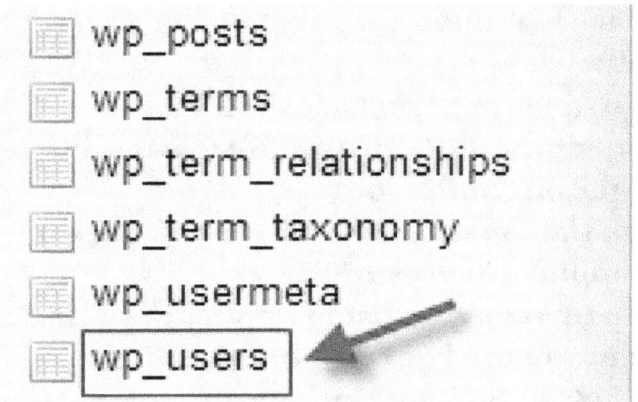

Photo Source: wexplorer.com

5. You will see all your usernames and passwords.

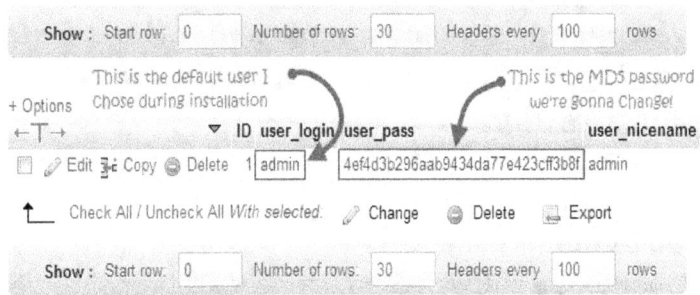

Photo Source: wpexplorer.com

6. Check the user "admin" to retrieve your WP admin password.

How to Back Up Your WordPress Site Using The Visual Installer Softaculous – This Stays On Your Hosting Account

Softaculous is a script library that automates the installation of open source and commercial applications to your website. Scripts found in softaculous are executed from the admin area of the site control panel via an interface tool like Plesk, H-Sphere, DirectAdmin, InterWorx, and ISP manager.

You can use it to install over 50 apps on your website. You can also use it to back up your website.

To do this:

1. *Go to your cPanel account.*
2. *Check the software and services section and click on "Softculous".*
3. *On the top area of your screen, click on "application installs".*
4. *Go through the list of applications and then click on the backup icon.*
5. *Click on Backup Database.*
6. *Then, click the "backup installation" button located at the bottom part of the screen.*
7. *A progress bar will appear on your screen. Then what's it's completed, you'll see a message saying that your backup was created successfully.*

To download the backup that you just created, you just have to follow these steps:

1. Go to your "cPanel".
2. Go into the software and services section and then, click on "softculous".
3. Click on the "backup and restore" link at the upper right portion of your screen.
4. Now, click on the file name of the backup that you created.

5. Once, you downloaded the backups you need, remove the backups that you no longer need. Clicking the "x" icon next to the file you want to remove.

How to Make A Multi-Site Network and Why This Can Be Super Useful For WorkGroups With Multiple Bloggers

Networking is important in any kind of business, even in blogging. WordPress allows you to create a network of websites using its "multisite" feature.

Creating a multi-site network is like creating your own "WordPress.com". This allows you to run as many sites as you want.

The multisite feature has a lot of benefits and applications. This feature comes in handy to companies who manages various brands. Let's say that you're a wellness company that sells honey, essential oil perfumes, sunblocks, and yoga mats. The WP multisite feature allows you to efficiently manage the website of each of your product line. You can also use it to create a network of bloggers.

Here's what you need to do to create a network within your WordPress site:

1. Prepare your WP site before you enable the multisite feature. This is because your website will be updated once you create a network. So, it is wise to backup your files. You also need to deactivate your active plugins. You can reactivate them after you create the multisite network.

2. Enable the multisite feature in your wp-config.php file. Open the file and add this code above the first line:
/*Multisite*/
Define ('WP_ALLOW_MULTISITE', true);

You also have to adjust your memory settings in the PHP.INI file in your web host root directory to maximize your website load speed.

You'll often encounter the "exhausted memory error" when you're using WordPress or any other free open source PHP program. When you encounter this error, you need to change the memory limit in your php.ini file by following these steps:

1. Go to your "cPanel".
2. Go to the file section and look for the file manager.

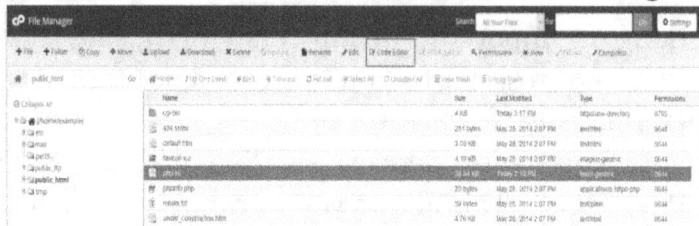

Photo Source: inmotionhosting.com

3. Select the PHP.INI file and then use the code editor to edit the file. Add this script:

memory_limit = 64M

Remember that the maximum memory that a script may consume is 64 MB, so make sure to set your memory limit to 64 MB.

4. Once you're done, click on "save changes.

How to Set Your WordPress Site To Auto-Update The Themes, Plugins, and Even When A New Version of WordPress Comes out

Keeping your website updated at all times increases the stability and security of your site. It also helps to take advantage of the cool features that comes with the latest version of WordPress. It also increases your website speed and fixes bugs.

To auto-update all your plugins whenever a new version of WordPress comes out, simply add this code to your site's specific plug in or php file:

add_filter('auto_update_plugin', '_return_true')

If you also want to auto-update your theme once a new version comes out, simply add this code:

add_filter('auto_update_theme', '_return_true')

WP also give you the option to do this in the softaculous dashboard within your cPanel account.

Resources

Fastest & Cheapest Wordpress VPS (Virtual Private Server) Hosting Plans
https://Internetweb.host

www.ingramcontent.com/pod-product-compliance
Lightning Source LLC
Chambersburg PA
CBHW071258220526
45468CB00001B/179